Life's Little Lessons Too, A Proper Life with a Career

James Smith

ISBN 978-1-68526-615-8 (Paperback)
ISBN 978-1-68526-616-5 (Digital)

Copyright © 2022 James Smith
All rights reserved
First Edition

All rights reserved. No part of this publication may be reproduced, distributed, or transmitted in any form or by any means, including photocopying, recording, or other electronic or mechanical methods without the prior written permission of the publisher. For permission requests, solicit the publisher via the address below.

Covenant Books
11661 Hwy 707
Murrells Inlet, SC 29576
www.covenantbooks.com

Contents

Foreword ix
Acknowledgments xiii
Introduction xvii
    Background xvii
    The Story xvii
    The Lesson xviii

1: Goal Setting 1
    Background 1
    The Discussion 2
    The Lesson 3

2: Focus on the Prize 5
    Personal Experience 5
    The Discussion 6
    The Lesson 8

3: Financial Security 9
    Personal Experience 9
    The Discussion 11
    A Financial Reality 12
    The Lesson 13

4: The Advertised Expert 15
    The Discussion 15
    Authority and Responsibility 16
    The Public Sector 17
    Personal Experience 19

    Lessons Learned 21
    The Current State 21
    What Is an Innovator? 23
    Helping the Innovator...24
    The Lesson 25

5: Age and Treachery 27
    The Discussion..27
    The Lesson 30

6: Jobs versus Wealth 33
    The Discussion..33
    The Needs of Innovation....................................34
    The Story 36
    Success Metrics...37
    The Lesson 39

7: Can't Never Done Nothing...................................41
    The Discussion..41
    The Lesson 42

8: Directed Action: Goals 45
    The Discussion..45
    The Story 46
    The Lesson 47

9: You in Five Years..49
    The Discussion..49
    The Lesson 51

10: Knowing Your Direction....................................53
    The Discussion..53
    The Story 54
    The Lesson 56

11: Clawing to Success 57
    The Discussion..57

    The Story 57
    The Lesson 61

12: Three Types of Decisions 63
    The Discussion 63
    The Story 65
    The Lesson 68

13: My Admission 69
    The Discussion 69
    The Story 70
    The Lesson 71

14: Mankind and Energy: That's Why 73
    The Discussion 73
    The Story 74
    The Lesson 76

15: Workplace Friendships 79
    The Discussion 79
    The Explanation 80
    The Story 83
    The Lesson 84

16: Find the Cure 85
    Personal Experience 85
    The Discussion 86
    The Lesson 89

17: Energy: Our Economic Indicator 91
    Personal Experience 91
    The Discussion 92
    The Lesson 94

18: The Missing Link 95
    The Discussion 95
    The Lesson 96

19: Is There Anything New? 97
  Personal Experience 97
  The Discussion 98
  The Lesson 102

20: What Are They against This Time? 103
  The Discussion 103
  Possible Solutions 105
  Developed Social Orders 107
  The Story 108
  The Lesson 109

21: It's Not What You Don't Know 111
  The Discussion 111
  The Story 112
  The Lesson 113

22: Innovation: Will You See It 115
  The Issue 115
  The Discussion 116
  The Lesson 120

23: Changing Cycles 121
  The Discussion 121
  Those Other Cycles 123
  The Lesson 125

24: Science and Technology 127
  The Discussion 127
  The Lesson 129

25: The Virtual Commercialization Model 131
  The Discussion 131
  The Lesson 133

26: Too Many Words 135
  The Discussion 135

    The Story 137
    The Lesson 138
    Practice Activity 138

27: Stop Doing Stupid 141
    The Discussion 141
    The Human Story 143
    The Story 144
    The Lesson 149

28: The Innovation/Leadership Impulse 153
    The Discussion 153
    The Explanation 156
    The Solution Cycle 157
    The Lesson 159
    Leadership 159

29: Managing Committees 161
    The Discussion 161
    The Explanation 163
    The Lesson 165

30: Economic Indicators 167
    The Discussion 167
    The Role of Innovation 169
    Embracing Change 171
    The Lesson 173

31: Future Mobility Drivers 175
    Personal Experience 175
    The Discussion 175
    Energy and Mobility 177
    Free Enterprise and Mobility 179
    The Economics of Change 181
    Domestic Energy Sources 183
    The Lesson 183

32: Never Quit When You Are Down 185
- The Discussion 185
- The Story 187
- The Lesson 189

33: The Role of Scientists and Engineers 191
- Personal Experience 191
- The Summary 192
- The Discussion 194
- Price of Progress 195
- Embracing Change 196
- Arguable Characteristics 197
- Innovation and Leadership Value 198
- The Fuss over Innovation 199
- Roadblocks to Our Future 200
- Fixing the Problems 201
- The Innovation/Leadership Challenge 202
- The Lesson 203

34: My Failed Retirement 205
- The Discussion 205
- The Lesson 207

Epilogue 209
- Discussion 209
- Lesson Takeaways 210
- Closure 216

Foreword

The more I try to learn,
The less I realize I know.
If I should live long enough,
I will have learned only a little,
But I will have become wiser for it.

The title of this book, *Life's Little Lessons Too: A Proper Life with a Career*, is somewhat vague in the wording, and even more so in the intended meaning. Clearly, if the word *proper* was deleted, then the title would not beg an explanation. The definition of the word *proper* is varied, but essentially, it means something, or someone, that is considered socially acceptable and right. What, then, adds to the confusion in the definition is one person or group may have fixed notions of what is *proper*, while the next person or group will object to that understanding. Plus, each of these groups might be living amongst each other, and so who and what is *proper* can become contentious where each group, trying to be right, can become a stressor for all of the parties involved in contrast to simply learning to accommodate the others' ideas.

The reality is that in an ever-evolving and changing society that is comprised of numerous groups of unique individuals with differing cultural, religious, and ethnic backgrounds, the definition of *proper* can have a variety of definitions and meanings, and even more troublesome, those meanings can change due to internal shifts of what is acceptable today in contrast to what the accepted beliefs were from yesterday. More significantly, outside influences can have an even more dramatic impact on what we individually and collectively accept as *proper*.

Most of these definitions and their constantly changing differences can be easily illustrated in the changing style of the clothes we wear, the words and their definitions we use, plus the everyday choices we make in almost everything we do. Admittedly, some of these choices may not rise in importance to affect the definition of *proper* for that item or issue but collectively we are always impacted by what others around us believe and act upon, even if subtly.

Our ability to live with, and among, these many *proper* definitional differences is what will allow us to be successful and provide for a fulfilled lifestyle, but we do have to knowingly and willingly participate in reconciling those differences. Additionally, it is in those differences and the changes that will continuously crop up that will allow us as a societal group to accommodate the many changes that are the cornerstone of any progressive society.

The key here is to accept that life and the culture it organizes will change continuously and sometimes even cycle back, if the latest change in the definition of *proper* is not currently acceptable by the represented masses, or doesn't provide for a positive move forward in the social progress of the people represented.

It is important to note that there are natural cycles to certain ideas that can be easily illustrated if you watch the generational cycles in clothes and hair and even makeup styles. While these styles may be augmented uniquely from the previous time period, the underlying style is often much the same.

Also, in the "art imitates life versus life imitates art" argument, we often find the influencer is the artist. In all of these actions and activities, there are a common set of beliefs that are seemingly acceptable to all of the participants. It is in these accepted actions and activities where the problems often get created when art does not imitate the life we want and often require.

It seems to be much easier to look at the physical changes in our social order than it is to do a deep dive into what the organizing principles are that allows the culture to function in the first place, either good and bad, or effectively and ineffectively. Since life has never been simply a black-and-white issue, it is on the grey portion of the spectrum where the nuances of good and bad are laid out and defined. Plus, when it comes to being effective, life is anything but efficient.

It is easy to argue over style and use of clothes or language and its word meaning, but when it comes to more basic actions and activities like innovation and management or leadership and governance, these discussions and definitions seem to allow a broadening of the term *proper* to fit almost any scenario. Whether it is too ingrained or too difficult to sort out, or worse, there is too much vested personal interest in the current process, it seems there are certain *proper* realities that we are all affected by. If we don't learn to work with them, we will often become less than the successful individuals that we intended to become, or we might be excluded from boarding the success train all together.

Independent of the true value of the action or activity in current use, it is clear that unless you rise above the need for this usage of the term *proper* you will never be in a position to change those vague definitions of the term. To do this will require you as an individual to explore and understand the nuances of the culture you function in and to use those characteristics to better yourself and to work with those around you. Another important aspect to this effort will be your ability and willingness to accept or reject any of those characteristics that are a violation to your ethical and moral makeup.

This is the second book in an unexpected two-part series that speaks to the lessons I have learned during my short stay on this planet. The first book, *Life's Little Lessons—with Some Not So Little*, was focused on what I learned while growing up and how those lessons impacted my moral and ethical compass. Those lessons were then used with my children and effectively in the classes I taught for over four decades. While many of these lessons I learned from family, friends, and mentors, there was another set of lessons learned as a result of my interactions with the social order I lived and worked in. These later lessons came from my attempts to enhance our knowledge base, to develop technology, and to understand the nature of our universe and how we fit into that complex system. These later lessons resulted from my professional career development.

As I have written in the past, life is not performed in a vacuum. The individuals and organizations around you, plus the physical and social environment you live and work in, all impact who you are and who you will become, in some measure, and often in unexpected ways. Add to this the customs and courtesies, rules and regulations, and the acceptable and unacceptable practices presented by your social system, living life can become a very complex undertaking. It is in these interactions, though, where we learn to understand who we really are and how best we are to live and work in these changing environments.

Life usually provides us with numerous opportunities to learn what we need to become successful in our lives, if that is our intention. It is when we learn those lessons along with the total mix of the contents of those events that will affect us the most. It also might be the number of unrealized opportunities to learn from those lessons, when finally understood, that reinforces the importance of the event and how that lesson will impact us in the future.

The lessons provided in this book are basic to our socialization and how we will interact with our total social and physical environments. Each lesson will play out based on the individuals involved and the situation we are being placed in. While the situations may be unique, the lesson basics are effectively the same. Fortunately, if you don't get the lesson the first number of times it comes around, for whatever the reasons, it will continue to come around until you get it.

This book is a list of several of the lessons I needed to learn during my professional life, some of which I probably didn't learn well enough. It is not all of the lessons that I learned, but they are the ones I remember as being important to me at the time, where most have a story explaining the importance of the lesson that I experienced. It is my hope that these stories will provide some insight and help to better relate each of us together, no matter the contents of the story you experienced in learning your version of these same or similar lessons.

Acknowledgments

The reader is the reason this book was prepared.

The question that should be posed when writing a book is, where should a person start when acknowledging the contributions that made the contents of the book possible? For this written work, the contents are a compilation of experiences resulting during the development of my professional career, along with the life that conjoined that experience. Each of the events in this book, in their own way, became part of the collective total of who I have become professionally. As such, each of these events also contributed to my personal development and my nonwork life, often in very subtle but profound ways.

The stories, referred to as lessons in this book, cover events from the career development period of my life where some have happened as late as these past few years. Each of these events involved individuals that became unknowing contributors to the lessons that have served me well for decades. Each person and the unique situations and events we participated together in made the events singularly important in my professional development and how I currently perceive and react to the changing world around me.

Most of these lessons expanded my personal contacts and influences and added even further to my career experiences. Some of these contacts became lifelong cohorts and some even personal friends. Many more became personal mentors and professional associates. All of these individuals are due an acknowledgment for their contributions even if they never had a second thought as to the significance or value of that contribution.

The career phase of my life was what I spent four decades creating and performing. It might be argued that my total career path started while I was still in high school since some of the lessons and the work ethic was developed back then. These earlier lessons were all clearly instrumental in how I progressed in the later years, but this book is focused on the years after I became an engineer and then a professor. Those childhood lessons were covered in the earlier *Life's Little Lessons* book, which should be looked at, if for nothing else then at least, for the fun of it.

During this later adult time period, I gained an ever-expanding group of cohorts, mentors, and friends, with an even greater number of lessons that I needed to learn from them, which I then needed to teach as a means to pay forward.

Some of these more poignant events and activities are reflected in the stories in this book. Some are quite humorous since laughing at oneself is often the best teacher. Others are very serious, having an impact on my life and often the lives of the people around me. Some of these lessons haven't completely played out for humankind yet, and which will inevitably get acted on if our social progress is to continue in a positive and progressive fashion. I can only hope that some of these hard-earned lessons will add to that learning process.

All of the lessons are notable to at least me or they wouldn't have remained in my memories nor could they have become a part of this text. Some of these lessons regarding innovation, leadership, and energy are clearly not unique to my story; but these lessons may help the reader gain a different perspective on the importance of these survival changing issues.

Life tends to be cyclic, and thus, it is again my immediate family and friends plus the students and professionals I have had the opportunity to interact with, that have enriched my career-life experiences. All of the lessons outlined in this book, while only a portion of the influences that shaped my life, are the contributions made by those individuals that thought enough to take the time to influence me and for that I am grateful.

It would be unfair to not mention my wife, Sheri, and my four children, Steffanie, Jimmy, Justin, and Jonathan, in this acknowledgment, since they provided the forum to practice what I had learned earlier, and then from their reactions to the same, to then provide the counterpoint balance to the lesson's learned and then taught to my next group of contacts.

Finally, there are numerous individuals who have personally made contributions and have added value to my life and, through extension, this book. While they are too many to list here, the one that needs acknowledgment is David E. Bryte, who I need to personally acknowledge and thank. He has become one of my most important late-life mentors and a friend in my waning years. He is credited with, among other things, providing me with a place to be and a repurposing of my creative energies during my unsuccessful attempts at retirement, which has become another one of my hard-earned lessons.

Introduction

Everyone has a story to tell, no matter its length or its breath,
A story relentless in the telling with impression felt by all.

Background

This book consists of a series of stories that I call lessons, each of which helped to form my professional view of the world we live in. They also helped to provide the framework for the moral and ethical ruleset I practiced throughout both my personal and professional life. The stories are being told somewhat sequentially based on their occurrence, but they don't necessarily build on each other.

The stories relate primarily to what I learned as an engineering professional and as a teaching and research professor. A few of these stories are tightly interrelated to both my personal and professional life and were included in the earlier title, *Life's Little Lessons—with Some Not So Little*. These few will be retold here to help the reader understand at least part of the motivation for these later stories.

The Story

The stories are laid out starting from my graduation as an aerospace engineer and ending nearly at my current age, five decades later. The names of the participating parties have been omitted out of respect, and even some of the multiple story lines have been fused together to insure anonymity.

Each lesson will contain some background information and/or the details of the story and then a lesson that I learned from the experience. Each lesson will be based on that experience, although clearly, there may have been numerous prior experiences that I didn't fully understand, which could have contributed to those same stories. Alas, we are most likely all guilty of not getting the point at times, especially the first time.

It must be noted that my take on the lessons, most likely, are uniquely mine; and you, the reader, may choose a different understanding of the same lesson. This is, of course, as they say, the nature of the beast, which hopefully encourages and expands our abilities to function in our environment. How you reflect and integrate these same types of lessons for yourself will also be unique for just you, as they should be. Your age, maturity, and life experiences will hopefully help you see a connection to the stories presented here or one, which is equivalent to a similar experience. If it doesn't, then maybe it will in the future, or it may not.

The Lesson

There are several fundamental attributes and understandings that allow humans to live and work together. Each person will develop some form of most all of these as lessons, plus their personalized interpretations, based on their life experiences at that specific moment in time. Note that many of those understandings may change for them as their future develops since our view of the world constantly changes as we learn from and experience what we interact with.

While I am sure that there are other lessons more important to the reader than the ones in this book, I have listed these because they were important to me in their timeliness and content during my maturation and development as an engineering professional. Looking back during my years, I can see how they impacted me at that time and even more so today.

Hopefully, you can also identify the lessons that helped you become who you are now and what you will become in the future. These life lessons are important to everyone, and I suggest that looking back at the ones that moved you forward is an invaluable exercise. Plus, it will most likely make you smile in the remembering. Please read on for the first of the lessons from my professional career.

Goal Setting

Goal setting is intrinsic to our nature,
To have purpose, we must thrive to survive.

Background

Early in my professional career, as I was finishing up my first degree in engineering, I had a very influential professorial mentor who always asked what my goal was when he heard me say what I intended to do next. It became friendly bantering mostly, and after a while, I got his point particularly when my goal for doing something turned into a twenty-questions exercise through his unquenchable interest. It should be pointed out that his twenty questions always followed any statement of my next plan, including going to lunch or my next scheduled work assignment. The game, as he called it, became a challenge to me, and as he expected, I soon became very prepared for his group of questions, which soon became shorter and shorter since I was finally getting the message.

The message he was trying to convey was that without goals, how would we ever know if we accomplished anything or if it was even something that we wanted to accomplish in the first place. While I got pretty good at anticipating and fielding his questions on my daily goals, with a well-thought-out plan of action and an acceptable outcome, it became obvious that the lesson he was teaching me had long-range consequences.

After a while, his questions became more directed at my future life aspirations, and from there, the twenty questions started anew. I valued his help, friendship, and mentoring; and I miss his passing regularly especially when I come in contact with young people who announce what they think are complete goals for the activity they are currently working on. If they only knew…I pass this lesson on to you without the twenty questions, although you need to consider them and many more in the pursuit of your life's goals.

The Discussion

A popular definition for the term *goal* is that it is an idea of the required or desired future result that a person or a group of people envision, plan, and make commitments to achieve. It is also normally a part of that process to reach those goals within a finite time period, by setting a deadline. An expected addition to this process would be to set the operational procedures and rulesets that the individual(s) will operate under and also the final results that are expected when the goal is completed.

Conscious goal setting is tough for most people, although without much thought we set goals almost continuously as we move through our daily lives. We decide to go somewhere to pick up an item, and effectively, we have set goals with expected or required outcomes. Long-term goals that can affect your life or the lives around you are a little harder to develop or anticipate and often much more complex to create and pursue. These types of life goals need special attention to the details, plus the final expectations need to be clearly identified as the goal takes shape.

As with the fork in the road discussion, which can be found in this text under the "Three Types of Decisions" lesson, you will need to gage your success at each junction in your path to see which of your choices will contribute to the path you have set as your primary goal and which will not. Indecision will not get you to your desired developmental state and the wrong turn will be evident intuitively, or perhaps during your next personal performance review session.

Personal development, through goal setting, is a living and learning process, and if you are proactive in your decision-making process, you can go back and correct or modify any of your initial goal choices or decisions. One set of goals will not fit everybody and yours will change as you grow, mature, and develop. This will require you to customize your goals continuously as you live and practice the process. The key is to never waver from the larger life goals you have set and if you do deviate, to get back on track as quickly as possible.

It is important to note that you don't have to make correct decisions every time. Individuals often get frustrated and give up when they run afoul of their own lofty expectations. Focus on the ultimate outcome because your work and home environment will always test your patience until you have established the best habits and have encouraged the environment around you to allow for the new, more goal oriented you. A determined you will speed the process and encourage your environment to contribute to or, at a minimum, get out of your way.

Looking at any of your life goals, a conscious decision to deviate from the best path may go against the goal you have set, but let's face it, we all want and often need, to indulge once in a while. The difference here is that we know we made that conscious decision, and we will need to find a way to compensate for that enjoyable indiscretion by altering one of our other activities. This is what makes us who we are, where a strict regimen can be altered to provide a more joyful existence while still focusing on the larger ultimate picture.

Goals are like pieces in a puzzle that, when finally put together, will be that pictured you that you have set as your life goal. Like a puzzle, each piece will have a unique shape that will fit the one location that best describes you, and most likely only you.

The Lesson

Like any puzzle, the pieces that will finally constitute the makings of your life must all come together to fit properly for the image you require. Since you will ultimately decide on that image, and hopefully not settle for less in the end, your future and the path you are on should only be controlled by you as you are ultimately responsible for the outcome.

It is important that you understand that in the formation and shaping of each of those puzzle pieces, how and when they go together will also be important. Life is an ongoing, living process; and every action, or lack of one, contributes to that process. Additionally, you may, and most likely will, elect to improve or refine that image as you move through life's processes. Remember, you control the goals, pathway, and ultimately, the final image.

My mentor was very conscious in what he was trying to accomplish for me with his twenty questions, and I learned the lesson well. I have also tried to teach that same lesson to the many students and colleagues I have had occasion to work and visit with. It is this same lesson that I have used in working on projects and future research and development programs, plus the numerous planning committees I have been asked to participate on. This twenty-questions mentor clearly became, and I recognized and thanked him personally on numerous occasions for his contributions, a very important and influential person in my professional life.

Focus on the Prize

A wish and a goal are different endeavors;
The first proceeds from luck or grace,
While the latter from willful action.

Personal Experience

I finally recognized in my life that I did my best in the activities I worked on when I focused my intention, and thus my attention, on the required outcome. Sometimes, the intention was nebulas to me initially, but for the activities to become successful, it was the goal setting plus the outcome expectations that made the day. Stated another way, in order to be truly successful in the demands you place on yourself, you have to focus on the prize to the exclusion of most all of the daily distractions and annoyances going on all around you.

It wasn't until later in my life, unfortunately, that I fully understood the importance of this principle, and it has served me well since that realization, although it most likely helped me long before I fully understood the actual message. It seems even children can accomplish unimaginable tasks primarily because they can easily focus on something interesting to the exclusion of everything else around them. The key is to use this process for all of your goals, even if the required tasks to succeed at these goals aren't personally interesting, but are important nonetheless.

What I learned in this process is that with the correct goal and a commitment to complete that goal in a well-defined time period and with reasonable and acceptable outcomes, almost anything is possible. Thus, I pass on to my readers the discussion that follows.

The Discussion

One of the toughest ideas to comprehend and accept by any individual is the notion that you can do, and become, almost anything you put your mind to; this is essentially a no-limit world if that is what you intend. There are countless written stories of the underdog that wins in the end or movies depicting the "less than gifted" person finding their inner strength and rising to the top of their game, beating even the more capable adversary.

In these example situations, the theme is typically based on a major survival struggle or a personal trial of some making. Most of life's challenges are not necessarily survival-based, and some may not even be regarded as challenges of any significance for you at your point in life. Whatever the theme, though, almost anybody can live their dreams if they have developed the correct skills and proper intentions. The reality is that you can rise to almost any occasion where the key word is *you*. If you have the proper intention and you are willing to follow through with those intentions, the world is there for your taking.

The other difficult understanding is that we are often put into situations where simple choices, or decisions, unknowingly affect our future life goals and our intended direction going forward. These every day and innocuous decisions are normally not survival-based, but they often become important when added together. In other words, always pay attention to decisions you make, even the simple choices, when combined, can impact the path to your future goals.

Sometimes, even more importantly, it is the decisions that we failed to make that affects our life goals the most. It is easier sometimes to just let things happen because the time and energy to make a decision seems too much for the value represented by the choices. This is your life, and you should always have a say in what you will do and what you will allow to happen to you. Having a goal-directed life means you are active in all aspects of your life, including those issues that seem to be acceptable to everyone else around you but maybe shouldn't be to you.

Some of these decisions may even seem minuscule at the time, but collectively they can, and do, affect and shape your future path. Put another way, the seemingly small distractions or those insignificant decisions contrary to our goal-based intentions can collectively alter and possibly derail our future plans. Thus, we must be ever vigilant with our goals and intentions.

It goes without saying that no one is immune from life's distractions and its struggles. These struggles can often lead to a person choosing a uniquely different path than they were currently on or even the one they originally intended and have now given up on. Wouldn't it be better if all of those decisions fit a well thought out plan going forward?

The result of choosing your own path can result in an unbelievable and meteoric rise to whatever goal you selected, which usually only occurs with proper focus and intention. This is, of course, in contrast to reacting to everyday crises with no plan in place. The real question should be, can the correct and intended focus lead to the better path, thus avoiding the everyday crisis that made the reaction necessary initially? The answer is normally yes.

A life struggle or personal crisis isn't a prerequisite to someone stepping up to seize the day. While it makes for a great story, it is also the more stressful track to success. Being proactive and getting ahead of the problem is a much clearer and healthier way to use your inherent life skills.

There is enough stress in our lives without asking for more. By being proactive and taking charge of your future, the levels of stress and anxiety will be greatly reduced compared to the normal reactive approach that most individuals use.

Focused goals, that are personally chosen, then becomes the true personal vision the participant has for himself or herself. Everyone has a path in life; some directed by others and the situations around them and some by their own vision of their intended future. Once invoked by the individual, a well-defined path is the essential motivation and pathway to reach those future goals. You are individually already on a path to your future. The question becomes, is it the path picked for you by external conditions, or the one you aspire to and thus demand?

One of the most prominent results from any goal setting activity, the focus of this lesson, is the development of what, for many, will be their latent leadership skills. This will include the ability to focus on your intended vision despite the normal distractions and annoyances of everyday life.

This activity will also identify any gaps that require the development of specialized skills that are needed to traverse the best, most beneficial and expedient path through the minefield that life forces us to navigate through.

Finally, another interesting characteristic of those self-driven individuals who you will encounter in your life journey is the wake they tend to create behind themselves as they cut the shortest and most efficient path to their selected finish line and intended goal. As with most successful activities, others will notice and migrate to this focused individual to follow their newly created path. In addition to the willing followers that will help get them to where they want to go, there will be those others with similar aspirations that will need to be mentored, thus leading by example.

The Lesson

The distinguishing difference between the planned and unplanned lifestyles, often centers around goal setting and an unerring focus on the prize by the participant. The less capably equipped and prepared individual is normally at odds with the more capable or better equipped, but with perseverance and a well-developed goal set, even the unexpected individual can often beat the best.

In these situations, it is the individual's ability to establish goals and create an undaunted focus that will be the key to success. Focus on the prize, be vigilant in your approach to solving life's problems by avoiding or ignoring its many distractions, and make it your intent to seize the day at every turn for the rest of your life. It is your choice, and it has been shown historically that the person with a goal will always progress further than the one who lets life direct them.

Financial Security

*If you are not pleased with
The amount of your portion,
Then make the pie bigger.*

Personal Experience

One of the continuous concerns I have had throughout my life, and even more focused during my married life, is the state of my financial condition. It goes without saying that as the current sole breadwinner in my family, this is one concern that can't be ignored. More importantly, as you add children to the mix, financial concerns can become an overarching concern. I found this out very early in my life in almost every activity I became involved in and even more so as my years, commitments, and obligations have increased.

From mowing lawns, working around my community doing a host of odd jobs, and even the occasional delivering of newspapers, as a youth, I was very conscious even then of my financial condition and the hopeful promises I might achieve in the future, if I tended to the health of that condition. I suspect this concern is the same for almost everyone who can be regarded as a working stiff. Note, that financial concerns have never left the running commentary in my mind, and even with retirement, it is a continuous and open item for internal dialogue and reflection.

Coming from a meager upbringing, I was constantly encouraged in my early years to make more, spend less, and put the excess back for a rainy day. At that earlier time, I am not sure I understood the rainy-day concept, but it came from family and friends, so I accepted their advice and always put back a little. It is interesting to note that putting back the excess is still one of my active goals, but even with increasing income resulting from a professional career, the excess amounts, percentage-wise, are not much different than they were in my youth.

We seem as a population to always spend what we make, and sometimes we spend more. Most everyone has fallen prey to becoming a credit card junkie, so several decades ago, we, as a family, set as a goal not to use that means of financial insurance unless an emergency presented itself. I will say that this noncredit way of life has been most successful, although painful during times of perceived need, even when that need may have been less than critical. Let's face it: everyone likes to splurge once in a while. My children appear to have learned the credit card lesson better and much earlier than I did, so there is hope for the coming generations.

That little bit put back, during my high school years, added up to enough to get me through the first year of higher education. That, plus my reputation as a hard worker carried over from my youth, financed me through to graduation, doing a host of part-time jobs while I was also a student. All of these activities collectively served me well and eventually got me to the career I enjoyed for almost four decades.

In all of that time, especially after I decided to have a family, my financial condition always came to the forefront of other considerations. This was especially true during the first-of-the-month bill paying time, or when something essential in my life broke and needed repairs or replaced. All in all, while there were many lean times in my life, I always had a planned goal to correct any shortfalls, and thus, I extend this brief summary of what I learned, sometimes well, but mostly only adequately, in this lesson to each of you.

The Discussion

An example of a fundamental goal that will most likely face all of us is the condition of our finances and our financial well-being. It is always easy to say you want to be rich, but the definition of that term will most likely be uniquely different for each individual: where they live, how they were raised, and the current resources they have at their disposal.

For some, the term *being rich* means you have sufficient funds for enough food, protection from the environmental elements, and the ability to defend against predators, possibly with a small surplus for that often-referred-to rainy-day possibility. For others, being rich is having vast financial resources that can't be exhausted, even foolishly.

As you develop your life image, your financial health will become an important key goal requirement. As you might suspect, even defining financial health can be difficult. For instance, there is a sufficiency consideration for personal finances that says that you should require enough finances to have a comfortable life, keeping in mind the term *comfortable* can also have numerous definitions.

Goal-oriented individuals often establish a minimum financial security level where they can do most any reasonable activity, live well with access to standard medical services and recreational activities. They can travel and afford to visit and entertain others. They also have the resources to plan that next, even grander, change in their image. They will thus choose their career path accordingly, to provide assurances that this form of financial security is available to them.

Others set as their goal financial independence. This goal implies that their financial reserves are sufficient and independent of their career choices, the state of the economy, and the outside action or influence of others. Interestingly, this total spectrum of financial health is available to all of us, if that is your choice and intended goal. You, of course, must put together the proper visionary plan and be willing to stay on track to achieve that goal. Any location on the financial subsistence-to-independence spectrum is available to everyone, but it requires the execution of a well-developed and thought-out, goal-based vision.

For some individuals, to establish their financial goals may require them to seek that one lifetime career with guaranteed stability. It might alternately require them to accept that most career choices will not provide for financial independence without the associated risks of a nonpermanent form of employment.

You may need to use your visionary skills to anticipate market trends and future societal needs, so you can take advantage of evolving growth markets. Your visionary position may also provide the insight to create that next best invention or gamechanger technology, thus creating your own growth markets.

A Financial Reality

When finances are discussed, it might be important to consider the following. Some say that to become rich requires luck, inheritance, or the talents afforded to star athletes or prominent trial lawyers. The movies and written stories have sometimes indicated that to become rich means you have to cheat, steal, or sell illegal or prohibited products and consumables.

The reality is that, individuals all around you are gaining the level of financial success that they have intended, and they don't have to contend with the potential problems associated with some of the other less-than-ethical paths.

The choice is clearly yours, but if moral and ethical issues are part of your makeup, then the path is easy to follow. In other words, if your health, stressfulness, and the need for restful sleep are part of your plan, then your direction should be clear, stay away from the unethical and illegal paths. Set your goals or as a friend of mine always says: "Plan your work, work your plan."

Directed individuals are very plan-oriented and completion-directed. It is not a complex process, but it is one that requires your taking responsibility for both your decisions and actions, how you choose to spend your time, and the results you accomplish and are willing to acknowledge. This is goal-directed basics, and we have always had this success program built within our genes. We just need to enable it and then act on it with a focused plan.

At the end of each day (this same discussion applies to a week, month, year, or even your career) you have to decide whether you want to be the tail or the dog that does the wagging. Everyone around you has the same time period to work with and what you use that time for is your decision. The difference in any of the final outcomes will be your visionary plan and your willingness to act on it.

The Lesson

No matter the complaints, luck, waiting for providence to shine on you, or the seeking of the proverbial shortcut, the important realization is there are very successful individuals all around you who aren't complaining and who understand that shortcuts occur automatically when a well-executed goal-based plan is put into place.

The well-thought-out decisions, at the forks in the road, will provide the only shortcuts you will ever need. It will also provide the personal satisfaction that you made that decision, and you are the person who was responsibly in command of your path. It is on that path where your financial security will be realized. It is your choice, and ultimately, you are the person responsible for your choices.

As was alluded to earlier, each of us has the same number of hours in a day to work with. The time can be spent pretty much at your discretion. You can spend it dreaming about what you might have, or you can direct yourself to those desires. Many people simply assume they can't have the goals that they actually deserve and so they discount their accessibility and, thus, ultimately suffer the losses. An unfulfilled life can be very frustrating for an individual, along with the people all around you who often see your potential better than you do.

The Advertised Expert

All that glitters isn't gold.

The Discussion

Society, through its many public and private entities, runs at its best when competent individuals are put in charge and allowed to make responsible and authoritative decisions. At each level of management and sometimes leadership, the authority and responsibility grow with increasing levels in the positions within the organization. Normally, along with this increase in position comes an increase in a person's stature and responsibility, and often with an increase in the financial renumeration. This is the normal progression for an employee in corporate America.

Noting that even the best managers and leaders often make mistakes, as long as the errors in judgment and decisions along with the resulting impact are not catastrophic and the accomplishments on a cumulative scale tip in the positive direction, then all will, most likely, continue in a progressive fashion. Even the party responsible for the error may continue to maintain their current position of authority and responsibility, sometimes, though, with a little more oversight, at least for a while, from the higher-ups.

Placing responsible and competent individuals in positions of authority, though, can often be a haphazard process. The social system we function in is organized in a hierarchical fashion with those with the least amount of authority, and most often less responsibility, being managed by someone with a little more experience, or education and training, and with slightly more authority.

This higher-up individual is, in turn, managed and led similarly from loftier positions. Ultimately, all of these individuals report to the individual at the top, and as former President Harry S. Truman coined with his designated "the buck stops here" title—the president, chairman, boss, spouse, or in some cases, one of your parents.

In most business situations, a lot of directed learning and mentoring occurs for an individual to assume added responsibility and authority. This can come from prior experience, additional training, and hands-on mentoring. It also requires the individual to want, or need, to advance their position of authority and by assimilation assume the responsibilities that go with that position. For these individuals, the need to move up the authority, chain of command, is often an internal balance of desire, drive, willingness to serve, and what for a few others might be described as compulsive internal traits. In some cases, the desire to move up is based on a financial security issue as was discussed in the previous lesson.

In a perfect world, the authority and responsibility go hand in hand in some measure, where the individual becomes responsible for the decisions that they make. Sometimes this becomes a "trial by fire," but more often than not, there are competent "higher-ups" to use as a sounding board before diving off of the deep end of the pool with a decision that needs a little more rational thought and a lot more information—all part of the learning and personal maturation process. This is what some might call the normal and healthy management process where the business activity proceeds in a positive direction and sometimes solid leadership for the future is discovered and developed in the process.

Authority and Responsibility

What sometimes messes with this natural process are the situations where authority and responsibility don't go hand in hand. Consider the case where an individual has the authority to make decisions but isn't responsible for the outcome. This situation is often ripe with wanton misuse of authority, where the decisions might sometimes be made on a whim or in haste, in exchange for favors, or possibly out of spite. In these nonresponsible situations, it takes a very strong individual to not fall prey to the temptation to misuse their authoritative power.

Even in these situations, a healthy organization will eventually call to task a misuse of authority by imposing increasing levels of responsibilities. This either fixes the imbalance within the position or it eventually removes the individual, or that position, from the management hierarchy.

The other case can be just as imbalanced, where an individual is responsible for the decisions being made around them but with little or no authority to make a change or provide adjustments to the process. This situation can be devastating to anyone in these positions where constant, overt stress is the day-to-day condition and where most individuals in these situations don't last long enough to effect any meaningful changes to their work environment.

Some would call this a control issue, but in reality, anytime a person becomes responsible for the actions of others with no authority to mitigate the outcome, this then becomes a hopeless situation for that individual and the overall organization.

This, in a nutshell, is the day-to-day operational situation for most of the private sector and effectively the way we try to function in almost all of our relationships, both personal and contact situational. Clearly, too many bad decisions, or a situation that will not allow proper decisions to be vetted, will eventually ruin the business or the personal relationship in question. In other words, if the balance between responsibility and authority isn't in the correct measure supported throughout the decision-making chain of command, the opportunity will often fail, and the problem then becomes solved, albeit in a less than desirable manner.

The Public Sector

This most likely covers the majority of the activities we are involved with, or affected by, in our daily lives. The very visible exception is the public sector where our public officials, often called leaders, are elected or chosen as part of an election process. While it is clear there are some very competent individuals that get elected to these positions, by and large, most have little training or experience to conduct the efforts of the offices they are elected to. Even with all the rules and safeguards that we try to impose on these officials, the temptation for the misuse of authority appears to be a prevalent problem.

Add to this the lack of responsibility for the consequences of the decisions that are being made and the public sector is ripe for potential problems. More significantly, the decisions they make are usually long-term, and as such, they most likely won't be around as the identified party of that bad decision. Even if they are still around for the consequences, the system will either forget or forgive the error in judgment or even a misuse of power, at least some of the time.

This, in a nutshell, is the system that we live in and coincidentally the one we created and allow to continue to function, until it doesn't individually or in a collective fashion. Fortunately, there is a range in the amounts of inertia and momentum in any organized system, based on size, influence, and length of duration. A personal relationship might be considered at the lowest level, with a business at a higher level and the government at an even greater level.

The social order itself could be several orders of magnitude greater in inertia and momentum than the largest of these other entities. Greater even than the combined states of all the businesses and relationships. Using these terms figuratively, the larger and longer an organization has existed, the greater the momentum and the more change in inertia it will take to alter the speed and direction and/or to stop its progress.

We can watch from a distance or be entrenched in the myriad of activities in our social order, but for the most part, all we can affect in the overall process is to go with the flow or make changes that, at the beginning, might seem subtle but which could eventually have a significant impact.

Picture a large heavy ball rolling down a flat and smooth incline. Your contribution to the ball's direction and speed might be viewed insignificant, but if force is applied at one point always in the same direction, even that massive ball will be encouraged, with sufficient time to change, its speed and/or direction.

Add to your applied force the same contributions from other individuals, with the same intent, and surprisingly, changes will occur, albeit sometimes agonizingly slow. Note, that a system's inertia is also a safeguard against any disruptive faction bent on changing the status quo with little regard to the initial purpose of the original system.

Thus, the long pole in the tent remains such until need is determined to alter that state. All of this leads back to the initial discussion of the role people play in their lives and the responsibility and authority they receive as they function to make a contribution. The more important story is how we utilize and incorporate these roles in our lives. The following is one example of this situation.

Personal Experience

Decades ago, I decided to start a small business. It was a new concept in personal property protection, which received the accolades of everyone the program was exposed to. I was young and inexperienced in business and more so in understanding how to sort out what needed to get done, along with the potential sources of help available for my start-up.

Since it was an innovative new twist on protecting physical assets, it would require a significant effort in getting the word out, educating the potential users, plus performing the day-to-day operations of a new business. In this situation, I had the authority to make the day-to-day decisions and to ultimately be responsible for the outcome.

Numerous individuals indicated the availability of assistance both for financial and public relations support. Numerous programs were identified, manned, and operated by seemingly well-seasoned professionals with considerable notations on their resumes with an apparent solid pedigree in business. Some were private organizations, but most were supported through local, state, and federal programs.

Since this was an innovative program, it also qualified under several potential grant assistance and loan programs.

After several months of meetings and making presentations to the identified groups and program offices, the following became apparent: these individuals were elected or placed in positions outside of their experiences and capabilities. What always came from these individuals, and the offices they represented, were verbal promise of coaching and mentoring, often with financial support for the start-up and the service it was to provide.

The problem with all of these meetings and presentations, and the preparation and delivery of these presentations, was the significant expense in time and money needed to deliver all of them. The commitment was not the problem, but the failed results in receiving any assistance did become one. In all of these meetings, there was a total lack of consistencies in the messages being delivered by the different groups I visited.

Everyone seemed to have a different opinion as to what should be done and in what order. On top of that, the promises of financial support either never materialized or were not even adequate enough to offset the expenses in making the request for assistance presentations in the first place. These offices and programs were most often self-serving and with little or no experience in getting an innovation off the ground and into the consumer marketplace. They were under the direction of individuals with little or no successful experience in starting a new, innovative business. This, of course, was contrary to what was being touted and publicly professed.

In the private sector, the individuals came in two flavors: those who wanted to own your ideas and thus your business, or they didn't have the time to deal with a new upstart businessperson. Interestingly enough, the lesson was far from over back then. In turns out that there were, and are even more today, numerous individuals that want to help new enterprises and the individuals who create and champion them. These individuals, mentors, come in a variety of forms and with uniquely different backgrounds.

These individuals are normally not found in positions that are described as being there to help aspiring idea makers. They are the successful individuals who work quietly behind the scenes and help when they are properly asked or when they see something they can make a contribution to. They are not normally elected officials or post their credentials for public scrutiny.

They are the true entrepreneurs and innovators who want to encourage the same in everyone around them with a particular interest in those who also have the correct intentions like themselves. While they are sometimes hard to identify, they are clearly not the ones who are self-identified as the veteran businesspeople with the public positions to validate that claim.

Lessons Learned

There are a lot of uninitiated individuals speaking about innovative ideas and businesses. These are the individuals who fashion themselves as the intellectuals and future thinkers of our time but who have little or no visionary experience. These are the individuals who claim to see the changing future but often with little understanding of the fundamental requirements that must occur to realize that future.

These "wannabes" speak of themselves as visionaries but with little or no input or understandings into the changes that will be required to get to that future image. Once you set your intentions and seek the goals that will meet those intentions, you will become that visionary. Yes, it becomes that easy. The begged question would be why didn't these purported experts do the same?

The Current State

The word *innovation* is used to define a variety of concepts and processes. Most innovators define the term to mean the process of making an idea manifest. It is creating the invention, problem solution, etc., with the additional requirement of successfully placing it in the marketplace, the completed innovation process. Innovation can come in a variety of forms; but unless it recognizes a problem, need, or desire, plus provides a marketable solution, it is not an innovation. An innovation changes the way we perform life's functions.

Most of the current rhetoric on innovation is little more than a waste of time, often resulting in a false sense that the people who are brandishing the word actually know or understand the meaning. The true litmus test for the use of the word should be the demonstrable set of metrics that show economic value and a social improvement.

Thus, the cure for cancer, antigravity, or zero-point energy, as examples, each sitting on laboratory shelves are not innovations. They are a waste of intellectual capital (and to my way of thinking, a criminal act against society) until they go into the public sector and effect a change.

The problem isn't just with the use of the word; it also comes with those charged with creating innovation who have little or no concept of the necessary steps to bring about a positive, marketable result. Much like learning to swim, innovation is an experiential activity. While learning some of the fundamentals might ease the transition until you are fully immersed in the total problem-solving process you will quickly find yourself in the deep end of the pool with no lifeguard; remember, the commercial world is very unforgiving.

Thus, putting together teams of untried or unsuccessful professionals, no matter how technically trained and talented, to affect a strategy for creating innovation is, at best, a waste of time and money, and worse, a recipe for discouragement and disillusionment to the would-be innovators. If added to this are those individuals who have never run a business, let alone a start-up, created a product line, or negotiated a license deal, then the likelihood for a valuable outcome from the effort quickly approaches zero.

More importantly, those individuals who have the promise of an innovative future can be misled and even derailed by the good intentions of those who think they know the correct process steps to the introduction of an innovation.

What Is an Innovator?

Innovators are often regarded as problematic; they see things differently, and clearly, they march to a different drummer. They do not understand risk as a normal person might and the fire in the belly for their newfound passion is unquenchable. At least once a day, someone will tell them their idea will not work, it is doomed to failure, or ask them why they haven't considered the risk they are creating for their career and the future of their family.

The funny part is that this negativity gauntlet starts early, long before the idea gets close to the marketing stage. The number of negative comments and concerns goes up exponentially as the project progresses until there is a breakthrough in the commercialization efforts. By then, everyone will become supportive and claim to have contributed in some small fashion to the idea and the future success of the innovator.

Only a few game-changing innovations will actually see the light of day. Some ideas will not be strong enough or the organizational support deep enough, or maybe the timing was off just a little for them to become highly successful. Fortunately for us, their next innovation most likely will become successful as a result of the experience they have gained from the first go-around. Few innovators give up once they get the innovation fever and so a few setbacks only sharpen and strengthen their determination.

Innovators are the history-making visionaries and future thinkers that live among us. Sometimes, their innovations are so advanced that they have to wait for the rest of the world to catch up. There are numerous reasons for innovations to fail, but a portion of them always gets through, which then refreshes and grows our commercial marketplace. More importantly, even those innovators who do not succeed the first time will often come around again, sometimes teamed up with other innovators, and with something even better.

Helping the Innovator

So how do we help these innovative people and their ideas? It won't come from putting advisory groups or physical resources together administered by non-innovators. Remember, this process is experiential in nature; it won't come from reading books or case studies. It also won't help to get ideas and their creators up to the prototype stage unless they are willing to go the rest of the way to the marketplace. It turns out that getting the innovation and its champion through the proof-of-concept stage is only a small fraction of the process to successful commercialization, if that much.

What is needed is a dedicated group of proven innovators who have crawled, kicking and screaming, to commercial success. They can be hired or recruited as mentors to provide the direction and counseling for the upcoming innovators of tomorrow. More importantly, they will need access to the physical and financial resources needed to push their charges through to the end.

Plus, all of this has to happen without the typical oversight and political considerations that come from the way things are done today. If you want to encourage innovation, it will have to occur through an innovative change in the complete social and political system that supports it. In fact, it would be best if the political system would simply stay out of the innovation-to-commercialization efforts that go on continuously all around us from start to finish.

The innovation mentors that society needs are out there. Large percentages of them are either willing or are currently working silently to promote other innovators. Why don't they come forward publicly? It is because the current political and social system would manage them into obscurity. They know how to innovate; they don't just think they do.

More importantly, they have seen the vast potential all around themselves and how to make use of it. Most likely, they will keep working silently with the less experienced versions of themselves with the hope of creating that next great something for the future. If you are one of those future innovators, look around for that kindred spirit. Don't worry, they are out there looking for you also.

LIFE'S LITTLE LESSONS TOO, A PROPER LIFE WITH A CAREER

The Lesson

Authority in its best legal, ethical, and moral form should be respected and abided by; it is what allows the social system to function and progress. Personal stations and employment titles along with advertised program offices are not necessarily as they are represented. They are often the product of poorly thought out and wasteful decisions. In all cases, never settle for a cursory understanding of the roles and motivation of individuals in these positions. Always dig deeper, and if not satisfied with what you discover or realize, move on to the next potential opportunity. Opportunities are never-ending; it's what you do with them that matters.

Always respect those who assume responsibility for their decisions and actions. For those without the authority to change the process, it would seem appropriate to also have a little sympathy and to at least acknowledge their dilemma and possibly the pain they endure.

For those that assume the responsibility for the poor decisions of others, either they have no choice, or they have some personal problems that they need to deal with. They most likely will not be able to help you with your potential opportunity.

Finally, the new business example in this lesson was not successful. The resources of time and money both ran out long before success could be realized. At best, it was a good idea and the experience served me and my associates well in future endeavors. At worse, it was a waste of limited resources, that could have possibly been used better elsewhere. It is interesting to note that the experience, as painful as it was, had more check marks in the positive column than the negative one, but of course viewed only a long time after the fact.

The experience hardened me to the realities of the business world and, more importantly, in how to seek help from proper individuals and the services they represent. It appears there is no substitute for working through this process, at least not one that I have found. Either way, the experience and the support of others has helped me gain some successes in the marketplace. It has just taken most of a lifetime for me to get here. I guess I should have started earlier, and if I knew then what I know now, I might have performed better and earlier. Of course, if a frog had wings, he wouldn't be bumping his butt all of the time, would he?

Age and Treachery

Success is not an illusion; rather,
It is but one of your many choices.

The Discussion

Taking liberties with one of the sayings from David Mamet, "Age and treachery almost always wins out over youth and vigor." Those of us who are long in the tooth clearly understand the ideas behind these words. Having lived long enough, we tend to learn the tricks of the trade, where earned experience grants us certain privileges, partially at least, because we survived our past.

Mainly, though, it is because we, as living creatures, are always learning and have gained from the years we have spent here trying to get things accomplished. Through this maturation process, we have learned to identify the pitfalls and after countless attempts, sprinkled with a few gleaming successes, we have managed to track, often stumbling over, a path to success.

This matured experience is often overlooked by the casual observer. The more progressive and successful leader, or manager, always consults that experience and often relies on it to temper the reckless actions of youth that can precipitate from lofty designs, a change in the economy, new competition, or a change in leadership—in either a positive or negative direction. Experience comes from both the good actions and decisions, plus the not-so-good ones with the latter sometimes in the majority.

While we may all learn about the more positive results, success tends to speak for itself; it is the process of sorting through and culling out those less appropriate ideas and suggestions that normally wins the day. It is because of this that we recruit and train experienced personnel and then put them in positions of authority and responsibility.

This tends to be in contrast to the youth and vigor that was referenced earlier, or is it? The normal youth of any time period tend to be a little more restless and reckless, at least from the more mature viewpoint. They also tend to think of themselves as invincible. Their good attributes are normally aligned with a lot of useable energy and few obligations they have to be responsible for.

They want it now, and while they may have the vigor, they often tend to lack the tenacity to stay the course. Plus, they often do not have the financial reserves or the experience to know how to run what often turns out to be a complex effort. The worst part is they often don't know when to quit, change direction, or seek experienced help.

This often results in a personal loss of faith, self-worth within the individual, as measured against this most recent venture. This is, of course, in contrast to accepting this most recent effort as just being another part of the maturation process. For some youth, it takes years to recover from a personal failure, that when viewed in their later years, would then be regarded as a small part of the growth process.

This discussion has centered on defining two distinct groups separated by degrees of experience and, for the most part, years in service. It is clear that there are always exceptions to any rule, but by and large our culture, and the businesses that have sprung up from it, pretty much follow this dichotomy. We have placed our most experienced leaders and managers in positions of authority and through that process have created a well-oiled business machine that attempts to respond to the needs of our society along with the wants of their consumers.

It is with this experience that we have placed our future hopes, along with the resolution of problems that result from any ongoing and growing society. What has to be noted is that this experience came from the creation of problems that started with their generation. They lived through those problems, solved them, or worked around them. In some cases, the problems and opportunities were often ignored, or possibly the problems changed or were no longer on their current radar.

For whatever the reasons or outcomes, we are now asking this same aged experience to look to innovative solutions to the current problems of the day; problems that they may not yet understand or appreciate with solutions that, most likely, will change their comfort levels—not to mention, the implementation of these solutions may well come long after they are gone.

If we want to be innovative and to solve the problems of the current day and the near future, we need to look to the individuals that are living them, our inexperienced youth. It is with the youth that innovation will flourish, as it has always been in the past. It is with them that we must trust the future, hopefully tempered by the experiences of the more seasoned professionals.

The clever solutions and innovative programs that we are in desperate need of are not even being considered by the current establishment because they are too busy just staying ahead of their daily concerns; plus, they most likely wouldn't recognize the solution if it were given to them. The energy and creativeness that is needed to identify, solve, and implement the needed solutions is in abundant supply, if not excess, in our youth.

What this inexperienced youth needs are the advice and help that can come, in more than adequate supply, from our more mature professionals. This is what we use to call mentoring, a lost art in this country for almost a hundred years. In fact, take a look at our recent history and you decide if, just maybe, mentoring and the lack thereof might be a contributing factor to our current state of affairs. Keep in mind that the mentoring relationship is not to be confused with an apprenticeship. While both are useful, the latter is quite distinctive, which is often trade related and with a more formal program.

A review of most historical references from our noteworthy scientist, engineers, and business leaders normally contains a reference to one or more advisors and/or colleagues that were instrumental in organizing their new ideas and concepts, continuing through to the formation of breakthrough concepts and future businesses—what we refer to as innovation. These individuals were mentors, and even in today's society while some remain anonymous, they can have significant impact on their younger charges. Unfortunately, while the intent is pure, it is often difficult to match the needed help with the proper mentor. The real question should be why.

In today's information society, a person might think that the problem and the solution are just a few keystrokes away. The reality is, there is often too much information that hasn't been sorted through and can't be because the volume is growing faster than the inquirer can sort and absorb it.

It turns out this may be one of those cases where personal touch, a phone call, or even a contact passed from friend to friend will best fill the need. What is needed in this country are more localized grass roots efforts, similar to what we used to have and what the newly industrialized nations of the world are building toward.

In an increasing number of cities and communities across the nation, and around the world, there are organized groups of successful and age-tempered professionals that are offering up their talents and hard-won experiences to the youth of the area in hopes that these efforts will inspire innovative change, help with their charges' maturation process, and continue the legacy that they themselves have contributed to through their years of service. What is really noteworthy is that most of these efforts are on a volunteer basis. Some will even provide, or help find, financial support for those innovative projects and the individuals that created them.

The Lesson

Interestingly, it is not the well-organized, government-subsidized programs that are the most successful. Instead, it is the innovation programs organized through local civic groups and clubs, trade schools, and local universities; the key word here being local. It is the region that grows the talent and which also creates the opportunities. It is the locale that has its distinctive set of problems and needs and thus can direct the resources of its personnel to best fit the needs of the current population. It is the resulting wealth of the region that is then available to help that local economy continue to grow.

What's needed is to let these professionals pass on their skills and talents and to then provide the support where available to foster their charges' personal growth. We need to help them by creating and safeguarding networks where these relationships can flourish and then we need to help mainstream those ideas into the marketplace. We also need to not only support them with word and deed, but to also stay out of their way, making sure others do the same. It is with the more mature and experienced of us helping the younger individuals, with the energy and the improved vision of our future, that our successes will be realized.

Jobs versus Wealth

There is no scarcity in the field of abundance.

The Discussion

It is often unclear how critical the art and science of innovation is to the continued success of any progressive society. As the population grows in any social order, plus as the needs and desires of that population increases, there is a resultant need to constantly change the status quo. While the success of a species is dependent upon the survival of the individuals for at least long enough to extend the gene pool and to take care of and protect the latest maturing generation, the success of a social order is more related to growth and prosperity.

For humans, this requirement is the same as with other creatures, with the caveat that survival is only part of the process and creativity is yet another, along with many others. We are constantly pushing back the frontiers of science to enable us to survive better and to do so in a more enjoyable setting. We have conquered most of the less-than-hospitable regions of the world in our quest to create more and to be more for each other.

We have also managed to populate areas that by themselves would not support the local populace, relying on advanced technologies to support those living conditions. Some say the next step is to go into space and the surrounding planets and possibly in the future to reach out to the stars. It will be with innovation that any of this will become possible.

A short review of history demonstrates the countless times innovation has saved or at least improved the lot of mankind. Sometimes, it is through a slow and methodical progression. At other times, it is a sudden breakthrough that changes the direction and scope of our growth, often referred to as a gamechanger.

Either way, the change is normally recorded after the fact and often after the creator has left the scene. An innovation becomes such when it gets implemented by society. Therefore, it seems almost impossible to predict before the fact, the development of a successful innovation. If we could, then we could save on a lot of false starts.

The Needs of Innovation

Individuals and organizations alike speak to the need for innovation, but few would recognize it presented to them on a silver platter. New ideas and inventions are a dime a dozen and their long-term success is often unpredictable or slow to materialize. So it is easily understood how a profitable operation might steer away from unproven ideas. These same operations will reach out to clearly proven innovations, especially if those new ideas might potentially threaten their current bottom line.

Well-run organizations always work to cut costs and improve quality. These organizations are always looking to improve their bottom line but the potential for adverse risk becomes the deterrent to innovative thinking. From this stage, there is a natural reluctance to fix what appears isn't broken. Risk aversion often becomes the goal to the exclusion of any new ideas that might upset the current operation, even if those new ideas would dramatically improve the profit margins down the road a bit.

This is not to say that we aren't all trying to identify and nurture new ideas and concepts. The problem comes from trying to do so from the existing stage we all currently work from. In larger agencies and organizations, there is a tendency to fragment innovative efforts because each group clearly thinks they can do it best within the processes and programs that are currently familiar to them. The direct result is the creation of silos that academia, government, and corporate America have no single claim to.

To help with this discussion, we need to differentiate the definitions of invention from innovation. An invention is an idea. An innovation is the idea applied successfully. Numerous programs locate and identify inventors and their inventions, but few follow those same ideas to market. Note, that inventions are a dime a dozen, while innovations, the toughest piece of the puzzle, drives our economy and social network forward. Some of the more innovative technologies, especially those considered to be gamechangers, will spring from the science and engineering disciplines, but each new innovation will require the blending together of several nontechnical disciplines to become successful.

The programs that are ultimately successful recognize that the rule set for what works today could, in fact, deter or snuff out innovation for tomorrow. The solution is to recognize that individuals doing great in their current jobs are those same people less likely to recognize and develop innovative changes. That's why when formal efforts are established to foster innovation within well-oiled organizations, there is seldom any long-term market value created, or at least a lot less than there should be.

Most of these efforts are self-measured as successful against standards that are part of their organizers' existing wheelhouse. What you get as a result of this are a large number of ideas, an improvement in the skill set of some of the participants, but little, if any change in the innovation environment of the overall organization.

The most successful innovation operation is one that is almost completely divorced from the parent organization, populated by individuals with no clear affinity to the way things are being done currently. Of course, these independent operations have their own set of problems, some of which are accountability and reportability.

This independent isolation is, most likely, the preferred approach, but one that can be fraught with interruptions, interference, and demanded delivery expectations with deadlines. It takes a long time to create this innovation environment, plus the problems in finding the right people and the financial resources to achieve any kind of success. Even with this approach, there is no guarantee that there will be sufficient innovation generated to justify the investment or to satisfy the leadership that originally spearheaded this effort.

Most likely, there may be significant innovation created in this stand-alone arrangement, but possibly none that will appeal to the parent organization. This approach is regarded by most as expensive and unproductive until, of course, any of the results dramatically increases the bottom line for the organization.

The Story

Other than in-house innovation operations, there are numerous groups and organizations that promote new inventions as their charter to identify the latest potential innovation. Most of these innovation efforts are competitions that look for that innovator or entrepreneur who just needs a little help to get that next grand idea from concept to prototype, and then hopefully to market. These programs are advertised for general entrepreneurial use, but the final selection process is often left in the hands of those least knowledgeable of any advanced technology or methodology and its potential future impact.

I have had the opportunity during my career to assist others in submitting technology ideas to several of these competitions. It was clear from the beginning that these competitions were not to bring an innovation to market. The financial purse for these events was barely able to compensate for the preparations needed to appear at these events. What it did provide was a focus on the technology presentation for the participants, some public confidence, plus some limited notoriety.

It was also hoped that someone in the audience might recognize the value of the proposition and take this fledgling idea under their wing supported, of course, by their checkbook. While finding an outside investor didn't happen to any of the teams I helped to prepare for the presentations, it did happen to some others in those same competitions.

I will note that several of my advised teams did place in these competitions and a few have gone on to the final phase of going to market. I have yet to see any connection to the value and novelty of the innovations and how they placed in the final rankings in the competition. All in all, there was a lot of value received by the participants individually but little, if any, for the actual commercialization of the innovation.

The selection process, thus, often goes to the slickest presentation or the prototype technology that has features most recognizable to the evaluators. This also means these same judges are less likely to know how to penetrate the market for the potential innovations they do select. Also, the winning technology most likely gets little more than a plaque, local accolades, some questionable business advice, and very little financial support to get to the next step.

The directors or managers of these efforts are themselves judged by metrics of success that have little connection to making changes in our economic sector. Thus, we often get what we pay for but not necessarily what we need, and clearly, the gamechangers can get lost in the shuffle.

Innovators and entrepreneurs, by their very persistence and sheer gall, who do make it into the marketplace, become poster children for the programs that seemed to spawn them, but most likely had little to do with their success. This problem isn't limited to any one sector. Those federal, state, and local governments that launch innovation programs also fall prey to these problems. Nontechnical people, who have no appreciation for the value of advanced innovations and how it works to create economic value, often staff them.

Success Metrics

They also resort to metrics that seem beneficial but are often self-serving and restrictive to truly innovative technologies. As an example, funds are always limited in these programs, so the view is to spread money among as many as possible. The thought is that this may increase the number of ideas identified and supported, which may thus identify a few more promising ones. But often, this method stifles or financially limits the best concepts that would have required more investment to even have a chance.

It turns out the metrics that should be used to determine success is also not understood by the creators of these innovation competitions. For instance, if the single most important metric for success of the competition is job creation, then food service jobs become an obvious hit. New restaurants, food trucks, and mom-and-pop shops become very attractive as winning candidates.

The result is often a large number of jobs created by these organizations that are minimum wage with a few blue-collar managers. While this may mean we eat a little better with more variety, it does very little to provide a gamechanger for the economy.

The better innovation evaluation programs are careful to avoid using job creation as the primary or single indicator for success. They look for the creation of new and advanced industrial and commercial changes that will move the economy forward. These metrics are often hard to identify and even harder to select from the candidate entries.

The true measure for the success of innovation is not just job creation; it's related to wealth creation. New technologies and processes allow for the creation of new organizations, with their needed employee salary ranges. It also provides the tax base from these workers and the taxable corporate profits that emerge, where the profits are normally used to grow the entity and feed the local social infrastructure.

The goal, therefore, for these sponsorship programs needs to be strongly directed to wealth generation. The metrics should be the number of inventions or ideas, devices, and processes taken to market: true innovation. In other words, the metrics should be the number of companies formed, the number of people employed, and the total of the profits against revenue generated.

Several innovative organizations, spread across the country, are using these wealth metrics as their sole reason for existence. Some are being very progressive and successful. Others may take a longer time to be successful as with true innovations.

The Lesson

Having said all of this, wealth creation draws out other creative people who might normally go unnoticed. The potential promise of financial independence is a strong draw to a lot of creative innovators. The currently used employment numbers model draws out small business developers, which, while important, often exclude the person with the game changing solution.

Each of us have lots of good ideas that could go to market and become innovations. The idea of job creation will never be as strong a draw as financial independence and wealth development. It is the success of the other innovators that will bring forth each of you to create the financial independence we all seek.

Most truly successful innovation evaluation programs seek two conditions in their participants: A good idea and the person behind it with a fire in the belly to make it happen. The number of these individuals in any population is not necessarily small. Finding them, though, becomes the critical effort. The individuals best suited to find them are typically of the same ilk, with technical or business backgrounds, some possibly regarded as eccentric, and highly motivated financially.

In other words, the very people we need to identify innovation, plus those individuals creating it, are the ones you are least likely to employ or listen to. A lot of our ridiculed innovators and visionaries will be put in our history books long after they pass on. There is no reason you can't be one of those all-important innovators that will lead us into a prosperous future, hopefully while you are still around to enjoy it. If only we had a crystal ball.

Can't Never Done Nothing

You can't or you won't.
The reality is, yes, you can.
If that is your intention.

The Discussion

The title of this lesson, in whatever form you most likely have heard it, is not new and in fact, as a young person, I heard it far too often. For those of you who haven't encountered some form of this adage, I suspect it is because your family and mentors didn't like using it, they were kinder to you, or you are truly gifted and never had any problems working through difficult situations. In my earliest years, my father added the question "You can't, or you won't" to the above litany.

Eventually, the second one became the go-to for him to use on me. Hearing the second one was a direct assault on my sensitivities. While the first I found easy to ignore, for a host of reasons and excuses, which he quickly learned and used against me. At least this is what I felt in those early years when I wanted everything to be easy, plus, why did I need to learn stuff that I might not ever need?

In fact, as the years passed, the second phrase was automatically evoked in my mind every time I heard the first one, or when I found something a little too difficult to handle directly out of the box, as another old saying goes. Seems I eventually became my own best tormentor. Looking back, I realize my father knew what he was doing when he planted this thought in my brain. He was all about decision making, and while the title of this lesson is definitive in what it tries to convey, the second saying requires a decision and an assignment of responsibility to yourself. It turns out almost everything new that we need to learn to do will most likely be difficult. More importantly, if we always seek to advance our individual capabilities, the tasks will also grow in complexity and difficulty.

This is all part of the learning process, and like muscle memory for an athlete, the more we learn, the more we can learn, even as it grows in complexity. You should easily note that as you mature and your skill set increases, some new tasks are much easier to tackle than it would have been for you in earlier years. Thus, the more you learn, the more you will be able to learn, easier and faster, and it has been shown that you will not reach a saturation point where your brain simply explodes because you put too much into it. Note that I tried this exploding brain excuse on my childhood influencers to no avail. I soon learned that the rolling of their eyes or their outright laughter meant this excuse was not going to work to make my life any easier.

What I learned back then was that if I wanted something, I was going to have to work for it. Even when I thought I would never be able to do a particularly difficult something, it turns out it was my intent and willingness to pay the price to achieve my goals that was actually in question. If you want something bad enough and you are willing to put forth the proper effort, you will most likely achieve your goals. It is that "can't versus won't" issue that becomes part of our development process in whatever form we use it, and more specifically, the form that one of our influencers might use to push us over the next greater hurtle in our life.

The Lesson

The sayings are simple, and the meanings should be clear, but possibly, the actual thoughts behind the two sayings are a little more abstract than it appears. Life is a wonderful opportunity, and as you age and mature, the value of that experience becomes clearer. The one thing we should try to avoid is the forfeiture of our rights to make a decision because the assignment is too difficult, or it will cut into the time we want to spend doing something more pleasurable. Note that the new skill set we decided not to learn could result in greater experiences down the road so you are the one that must decide.

It does not matter, in most cases, what we decide to do or not do as long as we understand that we are making that decision, and we are responsible for the outcome now, as well as in the future. Interestingly, if we understand and practice this principle, then in most cases, we will decide to always move on to the next learning process and skill set. The key is to never let your lack of understanding about who is ultimately responsible for a decision determine who and what you will become. Even more importantly, you never want to let someone else be the decision maker in your life. It will always result in frustration and disappointment if you let others decide your fate for you.

Directed Action: Goals

The present moment is not determined by
Consequences from the past, but rather
By a conscious intent to the future.

The Discussion

A person's "intent" can be a powerful tool in directing the actions necessary to reach future goals. It should be noted that the term *intent* has several definitions. Sometimes the term is used to indicate a possible future outcome should the stars line up or a person becomes very lucky. In other cases, it is what directs a person and their planned activities. The most general definition for this lesson centers on an aim or plan, or in this case, a goal. Note that goal setting and attention to intention are common themes in several of the lessons in this book. The attempt here is to provide a variety of different approaches to these concepts in hopes one or more of them will resonant with you, the reader.

A goal also becomes the thing that you plan to do or achieve as if it is an established determination to act in a certain way. It is evident that setting a goal should be very high on your personal development list and is one of the primary traits that successful individuals have, or need to focus on, early in their personal and professional development.

Intention is more than just this set of definitions, though. It becomes a state of awareness, a way to focus on a goal to the exclusion of the numerous detractors and distractions that plague us daily. It provides a consistency in the actions a person takes, and a way to better judge the decisions that are inevitably being forced on us from every aspect of our busy lives.

Once a goal is set, intention becomes the driving strength and force multiplier for the actions and decisions that need to be made. From this directive, outcomes can be evaluated and employed to better define the correct course for current and future actions.

The Story

As an example of this process, paying attention to one's intent is analogous to the planting of a food crop. The end-of-season goal is clear, but to get there requires the completion of several distinct operations and procedures. In this example, the operations are well-defined and any variance or failure to perform these actions will affect the quantities and quality of the harvest. For this scenario, the choices and consequences are relatively clear.

In establishing personal and professional goals, the decision-making requirements can appear to be conflicting at times. The reality is that if the goals are clearly defined and the process and decisions to accomplish those goals are equally well-defined, then the processes to reach those goals will be similar, albeit usually different for every individual based on the inputs and the expected outcomes. It is difficult, if not impossible to separate personal and professional goals since they are by necessity interwoven, and thus, in most cases, the goals have to reflect their connectivity.

Bringing us back to the farm example, the requirements to grow corn may be well-defined, but the process differences between growing corn in Iowa and the Sahara Desert are vastly different. The reality is that goals and the processes to get to the preferred end point define the actions and decision-making needed for success by the participant. Keep in mind the goals and processes will be uniquely influenced by an individual's past and current social and physical environments, along with the impact of their age, education, training, etc.

Additionally, once an individual has goals set in concrete, and the processes have been clearly defined, the required decisions will manifest themselves as choices that advance the progression to the goal, thereby earning a person's full attention. If the choice does not advance the goal, then the decision to abandon that particular pathway becomes self-evident. Just adhering to the decisions behind a goal and knowing which choice is the best one is a significant time saver, which in turn often reduces feelings of futility and frustration.

A positive choice that advances the objective also facilitates a quicker response to the next decision that accelerates progress, thus shortening the time to a point of success in achieving the goal. The immediate result for the participant is a well-defined and uncluttered pathway to the objective.

The subtle, initial outcome from this focused attention to intention is the acceleration in the personal and professional growth advancement of the individual. As your goal development process gains new momentum in you, your colleagues and friends will notice this focused direction. Everyone wants to be associated with a winner, especially one that has a clear path to continued success.

Clearly, the route to the decided result commenced by setting aggressive goals and then sticking to them in deference to the normal distractions that plague us all from time to time, with some happening on a daily, if not hourly, basis.

The Lesson

There are very few things in life more powerful than an individual with a directed goal. When a person sets aside as many as possible of the distractions that are a part of life's processes and decides to make decisions based primarily on personal goals, then life's distraction become of less importance, and often most of these annoyances will simply fade away. Identify your goals for life and then steer a path through the many obstacles to reach that goal. You will be surprised at the outcome of your efforts.

You in Five Years

> There is nothing more difficult to carry out,
> Nor more doubtful of success,
> Nor more dangerous to handle,
> Than to initiate a new order of things.
> —Niccolò Machiavelli

The Discussion

An innovative way to stimulate and refine the development of leadership skills, especially in our youth, is through their establishment of long-term personal goals. Then by building the required decision tree around what it will take to achieve those goals and carrying out a timely plan for success, the fundamental attributes of personal leadership are established.

This process also encourages the person to focus more intently on those important items of their plan, in deference to the normal distractions we all encounter in our everyday lives. This seems like a very simple process, and sometimes, it can be. In actuality, though, its implementation can be a little harder to accomplish for most people, at least at the beginning.

For example, I was often given the opportunity to work and teach numerous groups of students about this process. While this part of each lecture was brief by necessity since there was a myriad of content specifics that needed to be covered in these courses, with just a few minutes, each class period, the process was easily started.

So over the years, when given the opportunity, I would challenge these students to individually describe themselves in careful detail five years into the future.

Curiously, while some participants had links to potential future employment, not one could describe themselves just five years out. Few had any notion as to their next steps after graduation. None had any expectations as to what many of the next steps might need to be, or what role they might need to play in the required decision-making process for their future careers and personal lives.

Please note that the process that I requested them to use was not as simple as just composing a personal one-sentence or one-paragraph statement as a description of themselves. They were instructed to describe themselves with details ranging from their personal life activities through their professional life aspirations. This included their health and physical fitness goals, their family and living condition requirements, all the way down to their transportation preferences. This assignment normally occurred over small portions of multiple class periods with associated homework assignments.

They also needed to drill down into their professional aspirations, including the types of jobs along with the management and leadership skills they intended to acquire and master, plus the lifelong learning modules they intended to tackle to assist with their careers.

These additional assignments easily turned into several class periods, often requiring large group participation and discussion, mostly centered on what are the actual key characteristics that are needed to allow for a secure and personally satisfying lifestyle.

As the assignments developed, they were then asked to identify and categorize the myriad of activities and requirements that would be needed to meet those key characteristics. Group participation became essential, as before, in arriving at a personally generated list, where no two sets of characteristics and requirements were alike. It normally turned out, though, that there was a common set of attributes that the total group would agree on, but how and when each of these items would be accomplished would have to be individually established, as it clearly should be.

Finally, students were asked to provide order to these personal requirements with a timeline for completion of the listed tasks. Since many of the tasks were dependent on successful completion of other items in the total package, and on a timely basis, it became evident that waiting for the next prompt from school, job, family, or friends to take action was not going to net an acceptable or predictable outcome. These students needed to take responsibility for their own decision-making process.

These young people realized that they had floated by for years on the momentum of the individuals in front of them. All of them seemed to realize by the end of these exercises that at some point, they were going to have to take charge of their intended future once they established the details of that intention. More importantly, they began to realize that if they wanted more in their lives, it was going to require them to not only take charge, but also to become responsible for the potential outcomes of their decisions.

The Lesson

A personal vision for the future is possibly one of the strongest attributes that should be established early in a person's life and then acted on continuously for the rest of that life. The act of establishing that vision by itself leads the participant to look further into the future they want to affect.

This is one of many practices that can be used to help everyone, and especially our youth, to achieve their greatest unrealized potentials. What will it take for individuals to realize that they are the ones responsible for their own future, plus the decisions they make in directing that future?

10 Knowing Your Direction

If you can't foresee the future, then create it.

The Discussion

If you wanted to go from your bedroom to the living room in your home or apartment, the process should be quite simple; hopefully, you know it well, and it has a finite number of choices. At each hallway or stairwell juncture, you would choose the proper direction to arrive at the expected destination, most likely with the least number of steps, and within a predictable time frame.

Similarly, if you wanted to go to your favorite shopping center, you probably have a preferred travel method, and of course, the directions you will need to get you there with the least amount of travel and time expended. This travel process is, most likely, the same for most every destination you choose, and if it works well, then why consider another alternative, unless you find out that it might provide for a better outcome.

In these scenarios, the initial decision to change locations was caused by a need or desire. This, then, precipitated the decision-making process to identify the potential routes to reach the desired location. Seems like a rather simple and obvious approach with a well-practiced methodology.

If we know where we are going, then getting there becomes a less difficult task. The question might then become, what if you know where you are but are unclear where you are going? Plus, what if that unknown target location might be moving, and you might also find yourself forced to move, in time if not in space, independent of the target that you have yet to identify?

This can often be the situations we are faced with in life. We know where we are, and we might know where we would like to go in the future, but we are unclear how to get there, and worse, the end target might be moving, as is normally the case in life. Just when you think you know where you want to go, you find out it no longer exists or has changed in definition, requirements, and/or location.

This is particularly frustrating when you are denied access to that target due to some change in the set of requirements that you were unaware of, or they weren't spelled out well enough in the fine print, that no one ever reads.

It is often said that it's the journey and not the destination that is important. While that may be true to have joy in the moment, the reality may well also require a declared destination that helps with the many choices needed to negotiate life's many pathways. This is particularly true if you have a specific personal outcome or goal in mind.

Once you have the target location and the time set aside to get there, then how you get there has numerous permutations. There is never just one way to reach your goals, but there are most likely preferred ways. These preferred ways improve the odds of getting there within the allowed expectations, if the destination is clearly defined. In other words, if you have a properly defined set of personal goals.

The Story

Consider the following example. If you live in Chicago and decide that your next travel location is to be on the west coast, but the next day you find yourself in Pittsburgh and then in New York the following day, what does this say to everyone you have declared your path too, including yourself? The journey may have been eventful and enjoyable, but if the goal was the west coast as a step in a well-defined process, then there has been a delay and loss of momentum in your original plan.

Picking your destination or goal facilitates the decision-making process. At every juncture, the choice of direction is more easily made, and thus distractions are easier to ignore or overcome. Also, staying on track allows more time to focus on your directed journey and the added value you can obtain from the activities associated with that path. The person who declares their carefully chosen destination and stays on the most expedient path also benefits from the support of others along the way.

The disconnect of declaring one destination but going in a different or delayed direction is naturally disconcerting to most outside observers. They will often lose their confidence in your commitment and withdraw their support of your intentions, or in this case, a lack thereof. They will become impatient with you and have a more critical eye on your activities.

This is effectively the situation that the average person faces with regards to most any future period in their lives. We, as a populace, have grown accustomed to following those individuals that preceded us. The path that society provides for us is the publicly recommended pathway because it maintains a seemingly proper social balance based on what some unidentified decision-making group believes is important at that particular point in time.

Furthermore, as with any large-scale operation, there is an economy of scale that begs to standardize as many of the features and functions as possible, quite frankly, making it is easy for the participant to simply do what's expected. This results in a life-long acceptance that the system is smarter and more capable than any of its contributing members, which is clearly not the case if we consult the history books.

Adherence to the norm and acceptance of society's established processes effectively starts during our youth with our current educational system. To facilitate the information transferred to the maximum numbers of students at the least cost, the requirement becomes focused on the lesser achievers to ensure everyone accomplishes a minimum level of competency. The key here is that in this process, there are enough participants to continue the current programs established by society, which does not consider the importance of the individual, or the handling of any future changes that might be coming at us.

This level of competency is used to support the current needs of society, with little or no consideration regarding potential future social requirements or the visions of the individuals. Average designed systems, to ensure some baseline minimal competency, produce an average population that ensures all have some level of skill but neglects those that desire more. In all of this, the need for leadership, in combination with other innovation traits, are effectively ignored and sometimes discouraged.

The significance in this discussion is not what the current social system accomplishes; rather, it is what it fails to do by omission that can affect the long-term health of the social order and its participants. As history continually demonstrates, positive and often disruptive change comes from the most unlikely individuals. It is with those seemingly few historical figures that we have often trusted our fate, no matter how disruptive their contributions may have seemed at the time. It is with leadership that these individuals, or their colleagues, made manifest their ideas and history-changing events.

Individuals with a driven mission and a clearly intended outcome cause the energy levels of everyone around them to rise. The passion for their vision often results with enthusiastic backing or in the joining of others on this path to their vision. These colleagues, and resulting followers, sense the force of this conviction and commitment where everyone wants a chance to be on a winning team. This becomes the driving force behind setting goals and then staying on track to achieving them.

The Lesson

Life can be tough at times for everyone. The key takeaway from this lesson is that setting a goal and then creating a course of action to get you there is what is required to achieve the things in life that you must identify are important to you. Once you select your goals and have chosen the pathway to those goals, it is your responsibility to stay on course to that intended destination. All of this is in fact your choice, and you are ultimately responsible for the outcome. Pick your path. You will be the better for it.

Clawing to Success

*Don't let the illusion, or attraction, of perfection
get in the way of real progress.*

The Discussion

This next lesson is a little off of the beaten path and very unlike most of the others in this book. I have included it here as a footnote to remind the reader of the importance of distinguishing between needs and wants. This lesson also represents many decades of my commitment to working with students and other professionals, and thus, this is just one of those lessons I couldn't avoid providing to the reader.

Finally, for those of you suffering through this book, most of you will probably eventually learn, if you haven't already, that lifelong learning is not just another useless adage; it is, in fact, what we, as humans, must do. Thus, understanding this lesson may help you to get the most out of any of your future educational and training opportunities. So please bear with me and read on.

The Story

Some time back, I had the opportunity to hear a presentation on advanced education, the majority and theme of which I can't seem to remember, which left me with a somewhat profound enlightenment. Somewhere in that presentation, the statement was made that in a lot of cases the failure of a new activity, enterprise, or educational program is not from too little capital but, in fact, the opposite.

It seems that when you are capital rich, you tend to design, develop, or service what you want in contrast to providing what the customer needs. Scratching and clawing can tend to make us a better, more responsive listener, and not knowing where our next meal will come from, if it is to come at all, is an even greater motivator.

Interestingly, this line of reasoning was a little uncomfortable for me at the beginning of that presentation. Let's face it; we never want our loved ones, or ourselves for that matter, to need for anything, and we even try to satisfy their wants, within reason. While this effort to make life as easy as possible seems perfectly reasonable on the surface, somewhere deep in my gut, or in the cobwebbed recesses of my mind, is an opposing voice that just won't go away, all beginning from the words in that presentation.

Yes, I am sure that I spoiled my kids rotten, unless you ask them, of course. Plus, I don't want to criticize any social programs that clearly provide value to those that are in need. Instead, it is the "want" in this statement that I need to focus on, as I have over the last four decades of my professional life. *Want* and *need* are truly different and often at opposite ends of a spectrum.

I have spent most of my career at an educational institution with an awareness of the significance of the value and importance these institutions should play in the advancement of the local and regional economy. We prepare students in a variety of recognized disciplines to a minimum standard of competency in the hope that they will enter the marketplace and make a meaningful contribution to society.

The institution I retired from, as with the many others across the country and around the world, also provide service to a variety of organizations and operations outside of just teaching and training students. Add to this the considerable research base that most of these higher education institutions globally contribute to, along with the opportunity the students obtain by working in these advanced research areas, then what the public gets for their tax dollar is a great deal, but is it as good as it could be?

LIFE'S LITTLE LESSONS TOO, A PROPER LIFE WITH A CAREER

I would never want to represent that our colleges and universities are too highly supported, and in fact, the opposite is most likely true, at least for some parts of their mission. The issue is not the funding but rather the packaged product they provide for what they receive.

As with the initial provoking thoughts in that presentation, we have come to a place where developing the packaged products is more based on what the institutions want and not necessarily on what the customer needs. Instead of the best product at the best price, we are producing the greatest number of graduates, as long as they pass a minimum level of competency. Plus, the research and development contributions are often more directed to the personal interests of the faculty and the mission of the institution, in contrast to the problem-solving needs of the sponsor.

Note, it is now the general consensus by many that we have continuously lowered the proverbial bar of excellence for students, over the last few decades, to accommodate the perceived need to graduate greater numbers of students and to make our institutions rank better against a whole series of moving-target metrics.

As far as the research and development goes, we now seem to be more interested in how much funding we can get and how great and large our facilities can become in contrast to the potential value provided to the community that supports them. Little attention is paid to the actual customer, the deliverables, or to the overall social and financial impact of the effort. In addition, there is also little concern over accountability or the value and the responsiveness of the delivered products.

Let's face it: when the total amount of funding and number of publications plus the total number of graduates are the metrics and not the performance outcome of those products, or in some cases, even the completion of the work product, or the quality of the finished product, then what can we expect.

Some of the best and most talented minds in the world who work at our educational and research institutions are attracted by the lure of academic freedom and the hope of making a meaningful social contribution. These same people then find the only way to remain in that environment is to gain tenure and get promoted using the classical metrics mentioned above, none of which are necessarily related to the needs of the customer.

It is clear that the customers that obtain their personnel from these institutions have not had a significant say in the metrics. In fact, looking back now, I am surprised that the customers have continued to support this nonresponsive behavior, haven't become highly vocal, or have started to vote with their feet. Since we are working with their children is most likely one of the reasons for their continued patronage.

Maybe the institutions are convinced that we are the only game in town. Of course, there is the unspeakable notion that these future employees need more maturation away from their home environments and the comfort and security that they have been raised around, so the time they spend at college is an effective teaching tool and, in some cases, highly paid babysitting.

All in all, these institutions actually do a pretty good job, even if some of it is by accident or association. Most likely, it is a result of the goodwill of the professionals working in those environments who can't just do the minimum.

So what would it take to do a great job? What would raise the bar of excellence for their young charges and also increase the value of their products to their customers? The answer comes from the earlier comments; these institutions need to design and build what the customer needs and not what they think they want or, worse, what the institution wants.

That means less standardization and more customization. That also means that the institutions actually work with the customer and respond to their changing needs in a timely basis that ultimately helps their bottom line. Then when academia needs better funding and more resources, the need will be supported by all of the commercial sectors with an urgency, and not as something we should do if resources permit.

LIFE'S LITTLE LESSONS TOO, A PROPER LIFE WITH A CAREER

The Lesson

In all fairness, the students that these institutions help develop work very hard to earn their degrees and the faculty and staff that support them are just as committed as well as being highly under capitalized at the student/faculty levels. It is not the intention, commitment, or the facilities where the problems develop, it is the direction and the responsiveness to the needs of society that is often put into question.

If these institutions provide the best and most responsive education and research base, and also continue to raise the bar of excellence, the students will come, flourish, and all of the sectors of society will benefit. Additionally, the commercial sector will also let them get more involved with their developmental needs, especially if these institutions can learn to be responsive and accountable.

As a final thought, a majority of the students, some of the readership of this book, will come to advanced education and training short of the required resources, plus most that continue on for advanced degrees will work in laboratories that are less than ideal or on projects that are less than fully supported, but they will still complete their degrees and most of them will excel.

They will do this because they will do what is needed with dedicated faculty and staff and not what they or their institutions necessarily want. We should all look back at what we have held to be the dearest and most valued activities in our lives and careers. It probably came from working hard at what was needed and not just from the "want" department.

Three Types of Decisions

*Indecision will do far more damage, than
in choosing the incorrect path.*

The Discussion

One of the more frustrating events in life is to come to a decision on a particular problem, and then to be delayed or denied the opportunity to act on that situation using what you think is a well-thought-out process. We often feel this particular frustration in our early years when parents, guardians, teachers, or any other adult we have been entrusted to, makes a decision to not let us make a choice on an idea we have strong feelings about.

Looking back at my youth, some of those past decisions, their interference, redirection, or the simple but an emphatic *no* were most likely very appropriate. In some cases, they probably saved me some embarrassment or some harsh wear and tear on my body and/or a long drive to the hospital or, possibly, the morgue.

Let's face it, kids tend to have a short view of the reality and consequences of their decisions. That's what the older generation is here for, to protect us from ourselves while letting us learn at a pace that won't overwhelm or endanger us.

As we mature and age, and I realize the rate for both may not synch up at times with what is expected by the people around us, we are normally given the opportunity to make more of the decisions that can affect our lives. In addition to this allowed freedom, we tend to also get rather sneaky in finding numerous ways around their nos. Sometimes, the end result of our decision is good, and we get to shout out our one good decision in a row, or more likely they have to help us clean up the latest mess we have created. The other possibility is we can hide our bad decision, cover up, or delay the consequences with other equally questionable personal decisions.

Fortunately, the world and the environment we live in can be very forgiving at times, so the questionable decisions we make in our youth can be overlooked or integrated into the learning process we all suffer through, some of us more than others. As we mature and finally assume the total weight of the responsibilities for our actions and the resulting consequences, we tend to get better at seeing the long-range impact of our decisions and thus with some help, encouragement, and helpful oversight, we become productive members of our local community and society in general.

Well-thought-out decisions are a product of our maturity, training, education, and willingness to assume the responsibility for our actions. The not-so-well-thought-out decisions fall under luck, grace, or some injury to our bodies and often our egos. Since we are creatures of choice, we are constantly making decisions in everything that we do, good or bad. It happens in the way we live at home, how we interact in the relationships we are involved in, and where we work and play.

It is part of the living process and one that we often take for granted in the lives we live. We choose, or make decisions, almost continuously and even when we are asleep, or distracted with other thoughts and activities, the brain is mulling over the issues and problems of the day, looking for the often-subtle ways to help get to a best solution for us.

In most of these environments, and particularly so for work, decisions may also require the input of others in a chain of command. There is also a question of who will be responsible for the decisions that are to be made, and more importantly, any outcomes and consequences that may result. It turns out that the more people that get involved with a decision, the more complexity that can result.

Everyone sees the world and each situation differently, and each brings a different set of criteria and understanding to the table. These are all important, of course, as long as everyone is prepared at the time to make the best decision. Also, in any group there may be individuals who have a vested interest in a preferred outcome, independent of the best choice for that specific decision-making scenario.

We all make decisions, some that affect only us directly and some that affect others around us. Some are personal, which can be related to the people around us while others involve what we do with the organizations we deal with. In all of these situations, it is the effective decision-making process that is important, where the efficacy of that process is what allows our social order to work as well as it does. It is also the failure in that same decision-making process that directly inhibits our ability to function efficiently which retards the growth of us individually and our society generally.

The Story

I heard the following quote several decades ago, and it seemed to resonate to the core of my thought processes. It most likely was important at that time due to a series of frustrating meetings I was involved in that resulted in little or no decisions being made on a topic that was immensely important to me. After I heard the quote, I decided to focus my energies on making well-thought-out decisions in a timely manner and not to be the reason any group decisions didn't get made because of my lack of forethought and indecision.

Lawrence Peter (Yogi) Berra, a famous baseball player and coach, once said, "When you come to a fork in the road, take it!" On the surface, this quote seems obvious and maybe a little humorous. Without an intended goal, though, and the required attention to the decision-making details, there is the strong likelihood that when you come to that fork in the road you will not know which path is best to take, thus stalling your progress. More importantly, without an identified goal you wish to accomplish, and the consequences of the decisions related to that goal, you may fall into a state of indecision or become unaware of the decision that would most benefit your future.

Meanwhile, other individuals around you, with a clearer understanding of their goals and the effective use of the decision-making process may pass you by, putting you further behind your desired view because you have not made the conscious decision to follow your desired path. It seems Mr. Berra was trying to make an important point. Another way to explain the important issues in this decision-making process would be:

> There are three types of decisions: the correct one, the incorrect one, and the lack of one. The first, we celebrate; the second, we learn from; and the last we are to admonish, for it steals our spirit and delays, and sometimes denies, our progress.

Successful decision-making skills are developed in individuals who are committed to making timely decisions. These individuals have well-developed goals; they do their homework on the topic in question and have a defined process for ferreting out the important aspects of a situation. They have a vision of what can occur in their future and what may result from their decisions. Thus, they are always ready to take the fork in the road.

Good decision-makers realize that some of the choices they must make may not yield the results they hoped for, or needed, to reach their preferred destination. We are at our best when we become bold in our actions and successful decision-makers capitalize on this strategy. Note that even the best decision-makers make the wrong decisions once in a while. As a result of their goal setting guidelines and their decision-making process, these same individuals can more quickly identify and learn from their mistakes.

Others, without proper decision-making capabilities, often get caught up in indecisions caused from fearing the risks associated with making the wrong decision. This, then, causes them to continuously fall further behind their fellow travelers; it stalls projects and frustrates the other participants. The practiced decision-maker, even after making the adjustment of a wrong decision, now has the time to go back and repeat the effort, staying ahead of the crowded intersection of indecision at the forks in the road.

Only through embarking on this lifestyle-changing understanding of making timely and well-researched decisions, will decision-makers begin to believe and know that indecision will do far more damage than simply choosing the incorrect path. Because these decision-makers are now unreservedly racing toward their goals, they know that they have time to learn from their mistakes. There is still time to go back and repeat a decision if it is necessary.

Keep in mind that the individuals who couldn't make timely decisions are probably still at the fork in the road and will probably still be there long after you have moved on for the second time. Therefore, the only wrong decision now becomes the lack of one.

As a final note for this section, there is a clear difference between a haphazard decision and one that is made with a clear vision to the outcome, part of the proverbial "Haste makes waste" doctrine. If the latter is made with an intended outcome and based on doing the hard work of acquiring the needed information, then the decisions you make will never be haphazard; plus they will be yours to own, no matter the outcome.

So the "haste" in the above adage is not necessarily related to how long we deliberate on an idea. Instead, it is whether we seek out the relevant and needed information, apply a logical process to arrive at the best of the possible solutions, and then make an active and timely decision.

As we have seen in the past, some important decisions are not always correct, or the best, in the long run. Unfortunately, if we try to get all available information on a subject and wait even longer to let everyone weigh in, then the original problems grow or change, and opportunities are lost.

Waiting is not always best. Nor are the old adages and the justification for stalling a decision because of fear of making a mistake, the mitigation of liabilities, or because it is not in our personal best interests. The problems we face today are not generational. They are current, and by not solving them now, these problems will grow even larger.

Timely decisions are necessary for any progressive person, designated leadership, or organization, if they are to avert stalled problems and take advantage of timely opportunities. It is also clear that not all decisions are going to be the best ones. Some will later be regarded as less than optimal. No matter the outcome, as long as we celebrate the correct ones and learn from the less than perfect ones, life will continue to be progressive. It is the "no decision" that is the most worrisome and that causes the most damage.

For whatever the reasons, we are constantly reminded that it is not the number or severity of the problems that we must face, but the failure of those that have been given the opportunity to make the important decisions who are not rising to the occasion to fix them. As another old saying goes: "Lead, follow, or get out of the way."

The Lesson

The lesson is as simple as the previous quote:

> There are three types of decisions: the correct one, the incorrect one, and the lack of one. The first, we celebrate; the second, we learn from; and the last we are to admonish, for it steals our spirit and delays, and sometimes denies, our progress.

Do your homework on a topic and always be prepared to make a contribution and a decision. Do not let indecision stall your progress and diminish your personal view of the future.

13 My Admission

> Ah but a man's reach should exceed his grasp.
> —Robert Browning

The Discussion

Over the years, I have often been caught off guard by new scientific discoveries that were in direct conflict to those postulated realities that I had learned or been taught earlier in my career. I once took some time to review my old high school physics book and was startled by the inconsistencies I found when compared with the current scientific understandings of today.

I don't know why this was a surprise since our understandings and beliefs have constantly changed and evolved throughout history. It hasn't been that long since the Earth was flat, and the universe revolved around this planet. I guess I was surprised since it had only been a few decades since I was in high school and already what we know and believe has changed.

These changes, most likely, will continue to come at us and with increased frequency. The speed of communication has encouraged this, plus, the need to handle an ever-increasing number of social and environmental problems has mandated we need to learn more and do it faster. This increased pace is also required to stay ahead of the problems we create simply because we are here on this planet, plus there are more of us to deal with than at any other time in history.

Needless to say, the realization that what we knew as fact yesterday may have changed overnight made me feel a little uncomfortable. Let's face it, an educator does not want to teach incorrect principles even when the current ones feel comfortable and fit their personal view of the world. These same educators, also, don't want to teach principles and espouse on concepts that might change overnight.

My other concern was that my take on reality was impacted, or at least influenced, by what I previously believed and had learned experientially. The question then became, if I had learned a different principal or belief, would I have seen my reality differently. The answer was clearly a probable yes, maybe.

So why the uneasiness? The answer is most likely that we get comfortable with what we know and want to believe, and change can be a little disconcerting at times. We normally resist change, but as the old adage goes, the only constant in the universe is change. So I adjusted my style a little and decided to adopt the notion of change into my teachings.

The Story

Shortly after I had my not-so-remarkable realization that change was to be the only constant in our futures, I set about teaching students that what we know may only fit the reality that we see presently. That we, as professionals, need to assume that these principles and concepts are only based on what we currently know and understand, that the changes that will inevitably come might be either subtle or with a stark realization.

What was important was the need for us as scientists and engineers to understand this and expect it to occur unexpectedly. In fact, my intent was to encourage students to question what we know and understand and, more importantly, to take a second look at their reality in hopes of discovering new ways of doing things.

I reflect back on the open discussions we had in these classes and the remarkable technological progress that has been made by many of these same students. These discussions were often impromptu, and usually as a result of a question or a comment made on what they currently believed. It was at some later point in time that I prepared the notice provided below to be posted at the beginning of most of these classes as a means to start these classes off right. The notice said:

My Admission

Over the course of my long career, and specifically even more so now, I have come to accept, and thus need to come clean, two admissions regarding what I believe and have tried to convey in my classroom, laboratory, and personal life. First, when dealing with the real world, which has yet to be fully defined, half of what I have been teaching and practicing is incorrect. The second admission is that I don't know which half.

The Lesson

We should always question what we think we know, and more importantly, what others try to get us to believe they know. Their reality and yours, even when closely in sync, can still be significantly different. In the scientific regime, most everything we currently understand will get redefined or completely changed, even during our lifetimes. That is part of the scientific process, and as history has indicated, that process is accelerating.

On a personal basis, everyone's perception of their own reality and how they fit individually into the overall social process provides a potential for additional unexpected changes in direction. All of these redirections and redefinitions are part of the process of life and part of the reason we have been so successful as a species, even when it causes stress in almost everything else we do. Being plugged into this type of mindset will give a person an edge in solving the personal and societal problems of today and more importantly those on the horizon for tomorrow.

Mankind and Energy: That's Why

We are but specks of energy, all of which flows from the sun.

The Discussion

Ever since modern man's postulated humble beginnings in the Great Rift Valley, we have thrived as a species despite the many obstacles presented to, or thrown at, us. Our success is, for the most part, due to our drive to conserve, capture, and transform energy. Whether man was harnessing fire, inventing the wheel, or establishing the first farm, every singular, seemingly inconsequential move by our ancestors has paved the way for the survival of our species by expanding our control and use of the energy available all around us.

As a direct result of this drive, humans have experienced two main phenomena as our society has progressed from small tribes of hunter-gatherers, to larger agricultural communities, and eventually to the technology and manufacturing centric city-dwelling world we live in today. First, the successes of our ancestors have afforded us an increasingly comfortable lifestyle. It has extended our life expectancies, reduced our birth and accidental death rates all while we developed our global societies based on the successes and failures of the past.

Second, mankind, as an invasive species, has spread across the far reaches of the globe and has seen a steady growth in population because of the stability and personal security that technological advancements, and the power to drive them, have afforded us.

Population growth was the social security of the past, where large families provided for survivability and genetic security. Current predictors are indicating that population growth will most likely decrease and possibly reverse in the next one hundred years or so. Only time will tell, but clearly, the need for large families is on the decline, particularly in the more technologically developed regions of the world, where family and genetic security is less of a concern.

In other words, as survivability increases, the need for large families and population growth diminishes. As importantly, not worrying about where you will sleep or what you and your family will eat allows for the creative and inventive side of what makes us a successful species more accessible. This creative and inventive side of our existence further accelerates our social and economic development. We, as humans, are at our very best when we use our intellect and creative talents to solve problems.

The Story

It is thus evident that cultural and economic advances, mostly driven by the visionary few supported by the talents of a personally compelled leadership core, has impacted the overall global economy. While there is a lag in global transformational progress, the differentiation between the haves and the have-nots has and will continue to diminish. The progress may be slow, but it is still human progress, nonetheless, and the availability of energy and the information that rides on its backbone will continue to shrink the difference.

In terms of more recent history, the great strides in energy use made during the Industrial Revolution, and even more so today, have propelled mankind into uncharted territory in terms of societal development. During this historical period, people migrated from rural settlements, where they led a life of farming to urban housing developments to seek opportunities at newly established factories.

Factory work at that point in our history may have been hard, but it was often an improvement over eking out a living toiling in the soil. With the vagaries of the weather always in question on the family farm, it was often the case that a factory job represented a more secure future for the family unit.

The Industrial Revolution thus provided for a healthier and safer alternative to the family farm, which also made the larger commercial farm a financial reality. It now took fewer people to grow the needed food stuff for the population, which freed others to work the factories producing the goods and equipment needed by all of the citizens.

Due to this migration of people, the population density in towns and cities increased drastically. Before the Industrial Revolution, the world population growth rate was decreasing. After this time, it started to increase again, eventually leading to the highest growth rate ever at 2.1 percent in 1962.

At this point, the predecessors to modern computers were introduced to the public, signaling the beginning of the Information Age. All these advancements, of course, riding on the abundant availability of affordable energy.

According to figures provided by an article titled "World Population Growth" by Max Roser, Hannah Ritcher, and Esteban Ortiz-Ospina, for this more recent era, the current population growth has fallen and is predicted to drop to 0.1 percent by the year 2100, which will cause the world population to plateau and eventually decrease.

This decline in population is unprecedented because, previously, every technological breakthrough has been echoed by a population surge to support and take advantage of those changes. Further advances in the developed technology infrastructure have increased our survivability, and thus, the need for larger families has decreased. The workforce requirements per capita have also gone down through the use of intelligent machines and more efficient use of our resources.

Thus, the current trend indicating a decrease in overall population is most likely insightful, but bear in mind that all these projections are based on a future balance in human versus world resource use. The question thus becomes, can we even support life as we know it with a growing world population, a leveling of the playing fields for the haves and the have-nots against our current technological base.

It is with the acquisition and use of energy, its universal availability with the ever-growing availability of information, where humankind will continue to make its most dramatic technological advances. Most likely, all of this will be based around increases in personal security and a decreasing global population. Increased energy acquisition and its use should also provide the world with increases in our creative innovative breakthroughs, which will further our survivability and social development.

To allow those societal and technology advances to continue to enhance our global culture will require a change in the current sedentary mindset created by the illusion of comfort and familiarity. What's needed is a reach well past our grasp, akin to the drive and purpose created by the instinctual need for change that brought about the current series of human opportunities.

What's needed is a shift away from the mediocrity of the status quo to the next great human challenge; global energy availability at a cost that supports and encourages the next great series of technological and societal breakthroughs, all driven by the need for survival and flourished necessity.

The Lesson

There is only one world to support all of us and the environment we want to live in. If it is not for us, the people, then Mother Nature will determine the outcome on her own and we will have given up the right to have a vote on the outcome. While we have some limited impact on the world's environment, it is clear that to mitigate any of those negative factors will require a growing number of technological advances and breakthroughs. All of this, of course, will require the inexpensive and freely available access to energy and the information system that is powered through its use.

The lesson here can be summarized by a quote from Heraclitus who said, "The only constant in life is change." So when we become

LIFE'S LITTLE LESSONS TOO, A PROPER LIFE WITH A CAREER

complacent in our actions and see a reduced need for creative investment, we only lessen our ability to survive. We need to always push ourselves through hard work and an even greater acquisition of knowledge. It is through our increasing knowledge and the use of the energy around us that we will be able to continue our progress in the future.

Workplace Friendships

People often forget your good decisions,
But they seldom forget the bad ones.

The Discussion

Human relationships are complex to navigate, to say the least, and oftentimes even harder to understand. It is part of the human process to associate with others and sometimes to even isolate yourself from the ones you may like the best. Whatever the motive for any such association or lack thereof, it is often a mystery to the others around you once identified as such. Even with all of the complexities of human relationships, we tend to look for, and find, other individuals to associate with in a variety of formal and not-so-formal relationships. We seem to find solace in the location of a kindred spirit no matter the named relationship. Plus, over a lifetime, there will be definable relationships we will all cultivate, some lasting a lifetime while others maybe only due to a chance encounter.

Most people will define or name these relationships in some fashion as a way to better categorize and understand them. These definitions also make it easier for others to understand when described in that way. For example, the term *childhood friend* is easily understood although the significance of the relationship may not be easily described since it may have been of a short duration and only during a few adolescent years.

A childhood friend that you still visit with or end up with in a more permanent relationship like marriage is clearly a major difference. So very often just calling someone a friend, an acquaintance, or a partner is not a sufficient definition when describing a relationship to someone else or even to yourself since emotions often play an important part in the degrees of value assigned to a definition.

On top of this, it seems everyone defines relationship terms differently. One person's friend can be another's acquaintance or associate. A person using the word partner can mean a business partner, a partner in an activity, or a life partner such as a spouse. Somehow, we navigate through these definitions often only partially understanding the important nuances of the definition, or by gleaming the rest of the actual meaning from other cues in the conversation. Needless to say, this lesson is not specifically on how to define relationships. Instead it is more on what we expect and can deliver on, when we do form a relationship.

For this lesson, let's use the term *friend* as the cornerstone of our discussion. In this case, we will use friend to describe another individual who you have had more than a brief encounter. This friend is not a random acquaintance or the result of a chance meeting, like in a line at the grocery store or at a restaurant. It is someone you have had personal conversations with and who you can trust to keep your discussions private between the two, or more, of you.

At this point, the length of time you have known the individual is not significant since we all have established a friendship with someone we have only known for a relatively short period of time. We most likely also have friendships that have taken years, or a lifetime, to cultivate. This lesson is not on the definition, but rather, it is about what we expect to deliver and/or receive when we evoke the term, friend, particularly in the workplace.

The Explanation

During your professional career, you will most likely have jobs with titles that range anywhere from someone in the rank and file to any one of the many managerial positions, including boss, president, chairman, etc. In the midlevel ranks, you could occupy a position described as the boss, manager, foreman, and depending on the type of organization, a variety of descriptive subtitled positions, such as assistant or associate, etc.

Inevitably during your tenure at any position or at any job, you will encounter individuals that you develop an affinity to, sometimes even to the point of them becoming a friend as described above. For most individuals, a personal friend and a workplace friend are uniquely different, although that may not always be the case. These two environments need to be compared and contrasted, the workplace versus your personal life, to help clarify this discussion.

Outside-of-work friends are normally a result of familiarity, proximity, and shared or common relationships. Some of these relationships will endure for a host of personal reasons while others will stop or fade away with time. The ones that remain usually grow in intensity with time and familiarity and the personal touch that comes from being vulnerable and sharing with each other. Whether these friendships will endure will be determined by the shared value that the relationship brings to both parties. Since this friendship is most likely based on a sensed affinity and not on the convenience of the encounter, the parties will decide if what they are gaining is worth the price of time and energy needed to maintain the relationship.

This needs to be contrasted with friendships that develop at your place of employment. These friendships often develop because you are located together for long periods of time and on a schedule that is predictable. These individuals have a vested interest in getting along with each other if they are to perform their assignments to the satisfaction of their supervisors. It is often the case that these friendships are artificially contrived to get the most out of the job assignments although these relationships may seem solid and long-lasting.

What I have seen in a lot of cases is that the best of workplace friends, when they relocate to new locations, never make contact with each other again. While this may be surprising and possibly disappointing, the reality is that most of my colleagues, including me, have had extended conversations about this reality. I should point out that while I have missed seeing many of these workplace friends again, I only made half-hearted attempts to reestablish contact with them, as was the case for many of my associates and their workplace friends. This seems to be the nature of these relationships although we often have trouble accepting that.

It is often said that the exception proves the rule. There are a lot of workplace friends whose relationships have survived the test of time and relocation. As long as these friends are at approximately the same level in the management hierarchy, then they will enjoy their relationship and still provide value to the organization that employs them. Sometimes, though, a difference in their leadership ranks can impact their friendship, or the overall work environment they are trying to encourage.

For example, during periods of abnormal stress, people will identify others as having an easier job, or they are getting preferential treatment because of a friendship within the ranks. While it doesn't have to have a demonstratable basis, it turns out that perception can become the actual reality. So having a friend at higher levels within the organization can damage both careers and at least partially destroy the moral of the work environment for everybody.

I have seen situations where one or both of these friends have been forced to relocate to remove the stigma of their presumed preferential treatment. As with the above examples, some of these friendships fell apart with their moves, but others didn't. In fact, the ones that were good friends at the same job are still as close, if not closer, than before.

There is another side to the workplace friendship that needs to be discussed. I have often, as with most people, been asked to get a friend, or a friend's child, a job. This can be such a slippery slope since depending on your appreciation for the potential of the new employee and their perception of what the job entails, all of this can be a problem in the making. Since you have provided the recommendation you are forever linked to the new hire's performance. Depending on the respective management levels between you and the new hire this recommendation can impact the work environment of everyone between your two management levels.

If you are recommending someone for a temporary job where someone else can evaluate their performance for a future permanent job, then there is less liability. If, instead, you are recommending someone who will take on an important job with lots of responsibilities, then their performance will impact your performance directly and often in subtle ways. People often forget your good decisions, but they seldom forget the bad ones. In other words, be careful who you recommend even if they are friends. It could adversely affect your job and possibly destroy your friendship.

The Story

A friend in the workplace isn't always bad; it just needs to have a heightened amount of awareness, plus the potential consequences need to be managed properly. I give the following example that I was a party too.

When I was much younger, I had a job as an instructor in a university. I had been in this position for several years and enjoyed the teaching responsibilities while I completed my next engineering degree. As was the habit, the engineering department was constantly bringing in new people as students, graduate students, and support staff. The service staff were often mobile, as is the case at most universities, and they would use this job as a steppingstone to a better more permanent job. They may also be there because they were the working spouses of students working on college degrees.

I had the opportunity to work with one of these new hires on the preparation of class lectures and laboratory instructional aides. This staffer was exceptional at organizing the workload and staying on top of the scheduling. After a while, I started using these same skills to help manage some of my extramural activities. At that time, I was also working with two small businesses, and with this added help, we were making a major difference in getting the work completed.

It didn't take long before a friendship was formed, which has continued for years. In fact, we have been together for over four decades. We have raised four children together, and she was and is my best friend, and my wife. Goes to show that the exception proves the rule. I do need to point out that we were very careful in the workplace, and no one knew of our budding relationship. In fact, when she asked her boss, also my boss, for some time off and he wanted to know why, she simply said to get married.

His next question was to who, and when he found out it was me, he was shocked that he hadn't seen it coming. In fact, no one in the college knew we were a couple until we were married. As this lesson is trying to teach, we took great care to not let our friendship and budding personal relationship interfere with our jobs or to cause problems with the other employees. There are a lot of examples in the workplace where friendships have prevailed and many more where they didn't. You need to figure out why and how you will approach friendships in your workplace.

The Lesson

It is your job to understand the difference between friendships and workplace responsibilities. Most employees have a responsibility to their employer and to the family they need to support. It is seldom that a friendship will trump those responsibilities and you need to always keep that in mind. Never let friendship dictate the course of your future goals or your career. It turns out that true friends are just as concerned about your future and would not put you into a position where your job and career would be placed into question. At least none of my true friends would, nor have any of them in the past. I differentiate between an acquaintance and a friend and a work associate or buddy. You need to do the same to gain the most successes in your life.

Find the Cure

He who fixes his course to a star, changes not.

—L'DU

Personal Experience

I have had the unique opportunity to work in and make small technical contributions to several sectors affecting our economy. The primary ones are energy, its acquisition and use; the medical industry, equipment development and procedures; communications, hardware development; and mobility, powerplants and improvements in energy efficiencies. While the contributions were not at all great, they did add to the collective contributions of many others to help move us all forward, at least a little bit.

What resulted often from these efforts was the realization that we often looked for the solution to a symptom and not the actual problem. This realization and the subsequent clarification of the issues often redirected the efforts of everyone and sometimes the final solution to that original problem became the solution to other similar problems, and thus, progress was made.

This lesson is a clarification of that realization. Hopefully you, the reader, will appreciate the significance of the difference between the symptom and the actual problem and will use this lesson to reinforce your focus on always finding out what the actual problem is in contrast to simply tackling the symptoms. You may still have to treat the symptoms to maintain viability of the situation but knowing what the actual problem is means you can also work to find a more permanent remedy to the current situation, plus any similar ones that may develop in the future.

The Discussion

We are a society steeped in the habit, if not addiction, of identifying the symptoms of a problem and then committing our personal energies and fiscal resources to the management of those symptoms, only rarely taking the time to recognize and eliminate the original problem. It could be said that even the medical industry primarily manages symptoms with the hope that the original malady will not further exacerbate problems within the host until the immune system can take over and save the day.

Actual complete cures, except on the emergency care side of the equation, seem to be in short supply for whatever the reasons, but eventually, they will become available, as with the polio vaccine and some of the cancer treatments. Until then, we clearly benefit from treating those symptoms. Often, it is in those treatments where life can become enjoyable again.

Clearly for the medical situation, the patient may not have all of the necessary tools or the physical reserves to fix the problem, and so we can accelerate and extend the management of the symptoms to help effect a cure or at least allow the host to continue to survive. In most situations, though, it is the host that ultimately fixes the problem, or the person passes on from any of the myriad of critical illnesses that we humans have encountered.

Using this as an analogy, it should be our ultimate goal to determine the root causes of all of the problems we face and then to fix them, and not just continue to treat the symptoms. It should be noted that sometimes the symptoms are a result of the underlying problem or they may actually mask the problem, and thus, except for keeping the host alive and comfortable, there is no actual impact on the original problem from applying the treatment to a symptom.

It is noteworthy that a cure for all current or future diseases could reduce the size of the medical industry, much as steam power and the automobile effectively wiped out the blacksmith and carriage trades of yesteryear. Yes, we still need and use the older trades for a variety of applications, but they have, by and large, been replaced as mainstay industries.

The medical industry, though, as with many others, would always have an essential place since we seem to frequently find a way to hurt ourselves and others, and the environment we interact with is not always as hospitable as we would assume it to be. Plus, I have to assume that the creation of new ailments along with viruses and diseases hasn't run its course for this species and on this planet.

In fact, history is full of breakthroughs, disruptive technologies, and social reformations, which have refocused the direction and scope of not only industry but society itself, leaving in its wake an often-devastated segment of our economy and society. We even celebrate those historical events, independent of the local and sometimes regional impact. This is most likely the way it should be since the good of the many always outweighs the well-being of the few.

The US has a rich history of providing the preferred environment for new ideas, concepts, and technologies to cure the problems and not just to treat the symptoms; this environment is often referred to as free or private enterprise or free market capitalism. These innovative breakthroughs have been a constant source of inventive energies that have provided us with a standard of living much envied around the world.

It is the free enterprise nature of the social programs that we created that has allowed us to prosper and to provide the beacon for the rest of the world to follow and, in the recent past, to emulate. Now, the reality is that this country is lagging behind many others in most of the primary growth indicators, and thus, in the near future, we could be removed as the premier economic and social power of the past couple of centuries. Or possibly this snoozing giant will awaken again and reestablish its position of prominence. I know where my vote and hope will lay.

We have some of the brightest minds in the world, access to the required natural resources, and the financial wherewithal to compete with any other social order. We also have a long and continuous history of innovation and the development of the leadership needed to direct our industry and to be our forward-looking decision makers. So what happened?

What happened may parallel the earlier discussion. We have become a society focused on symptoms and, along with it, finger-pointing at who and what are causing our problems. In the recent past, we had the industrial, educational, and social infrastructure to match any rival. This has seemingly changed through a lowering of the bar for excellence and a lost failure to understand and reinforce the developmental history of this country and the cornerstone foundations that allowed us to flourish.

This is sometimes attributed to a sense of entitlement and a lack of personal responsibility. The reality is that the problems are there, but the general public would rather treat the symptoms than to tackle the actual problems that are stifling, if not killing, the patient. Like the medical example above, the patient, this country, may have run out of reserves and treating the symptoms will only exacerbate the actual problems.

This is not to say that like the earlier example, the medical industry is not looking for cures because they are, and they are getting better at it. This is also the case for the innovative leaders in every other segment of our society. The issue is the limited availability of these specialized individuals, the lack of timely support, and the often-outright interference they receive for their visionary efforts.

We seem to have lost our goal, vision, and excitement for the future; unless more comfort and less work are the only goals. Worse yet, we spend our time focusing on our shrinking abundance, or lack of economic equality, in contrast to solving problems and thus eliminating the symptoms. A scarcity mentality, and the governing process that always accompanies it, is never progressive because it starts with a false premise. Visionary individuals only see abundance, so scarcity never gets on their radar.

As an aside during some cloud-free night, you should go outside and look up. You then need to convince yourself that we live in a universe of scarcity. In fact, if you remove the myopic view that we tend to cultivate in our youth, you will find abundance all about you.

This is one of the principles I learned early in my career. If you are not content with the size of your share of the pie, make the pie larger.

A scarcity mentality means if you are to get more of the pie, you will need to take some from others. This results in conflict along with personal and social stress. If you make the pie larger, then you and everyone else has more. You become the hero and you have followers who have a vested interest in your future efforts. Work hard, work smart with a focused goal, and abundance will become your trademark.

Capitalism works, but only if the bar of excellence is raised constantly by the individuals who are pushing us forward through innovative breakthroughs, both in technologies and societal improvements. Stagnation is always the enemy of progress, and history clearly shows that progress is the only salvation for growth and prosperity.

Living on the edge of the comfort zone is what made this country great. While being on that edge does cause problems, with the few unwilling or unable to contribute, the excitement that comes with the changes that will inevitably come makes life an exciting prospect.

Going back to the original discussion, adding more rules and regulations in response to recognized symptoms in contrast to fixing the problems only means that the current way of doing business will be the only survivor, and we become the loser. The only constant in the universe is change, so if we don't at least adjust, or more importantly, make the needed forward-looking changes, then the current set of symptoms will deplete our reserves and make life a less than acceptable existence, plus the patient, in this case, our social order will cease to exist.

The Lesson

We need the breakthroughs and the disruptive technologies to fill the progress pipeline again. We need to expand that pipeline with the thoughts, ideas, and inspirations of our innovators and especially our young people who will then each have a reason and a say in what they learn and how they use it.

Everyone needs to become responsible for their own actions and decisions and for those with the proper authority, they need to feel even more responsible. Additionally, we need to ensure that the very governing and social programs we create at least know how to keep out of the way of progress that ultimately must come if we are to fix the ailments and not just treat the symptoms.

We also need all of this to occur as a natural response to the needs of our society and not be artificially induced by special interest groups, domestic and nondomestic conglomerates, or political and social factions. It turns out we are often our own worst enemy. As an old saying goes, there are no free lunches, and we need to pay for the life we enjoy by making it better for the next generation. We also need to do that now.

17
Energy: Our Economic Indicator

Yesterday's solutions are tomorrow's problems.
The gift of the present allows us to plan for both.

Personal Experience

As mentioned previously in this text, I have spent some of my professional life working in the energy field, trying to add value to a small group of advanced technologies. It is unclear whether any of my efforts have had any significant impact; history will have to serve to tell that tale. I have learned a lot, though, and have tried to impart that information to the many students and professionals I have been fortunate enough to have had contact with. The hope, of course, is that they will be able to use some of that information even if I didn't.

The most important aspects of what I have learned involves energy as a survival-driver. As history clearly shows, it is in the acquisition and use of energy that has allowed humankind to flourish in this world. It has increased our survival rate and propelled our creative thinking to topics that a hundred years ago would not have even been considered. We, and everything around us, consists of energy and how it is used determines the evolving direction and success of the world's living species.

The following lesson on energy is attached because it was such an important part of my professional career and, obviously, as it is in all of our lives. It speaks to energy independence, but the real story is in how this nation, and soon the world, will utilize the energy that is all around us. Please read on.

The Discussion

This nation is again at the crossroads of innovation and economic revitalization, hopefully another stage in a never-ending developmental saga. The not-so-recent discoveries in shale gas and oil that underlie the majority of our landscape and the more recent abilities to extract these energies, using advanced horizontal drilling technologies in combination with hydro-fracturing, has provided us with an opportunity unequalled in the last several decades.

This progress and the welcomed embrace provided by the industrial community, with increasing attention from the financial sectors, has placed us solidly on a path to economic recovery. This recovery is not just in our economy but also in the shared excitement and motivation of our workforce, the revitalization of our civic organizations and, more importantly, the involvement of our youth and their aspirations for the future—a seminal change-agent for the future.

Those initial regions, where exploration and extraction are being focused, have seen an increase in traffic and trade, the opening of dormant or under-utilized manufacturing facilities along with the use of the trained workforce, some of which have sat idle for years. The drill pipe and the transmission lines alone will create steel markets for decades to come.

It doesn't stop there, though. The workers and their tools will need to be transported and they will need to be fed and housed. Additional fleet vehicles and the transportation infrastructure to move them will need to be created and updated, along with the service and management that they will require.

More importantly, this new energy market and the products extracted from the raw gas will create jobs and put more money back into our economy, causing a rippling effect throughout our nation.

This will help to solidify and stabilize the middle class who purchases the majority of the goods and services that we all get at competitive prices due to volume production and sales.

It will increase the size of the tax base, also reducing the support payouts, without the need to increase the tax percentages, all of which provides for accelerated infrastructure improvements and an increase in our ability to provide the needed social services that are a trademark of a caring nation.

As the increased gas quantities become available, the larger volumes will be slated to the power and heavy manufacturing industries, where for many of the current facilities, planned upgrades to meet air quality standards have become prohibitively expensive for the producer and the consumer. The conversion to natural gas will allow for the continued use of some of these older plants, in many cases with improved air quality, at a cost that can be more easily absorbed and without an increase in outages, plants idling, and regulatory penalties.

All of this will, of course, take time, measured at least in years and most likely decades. Power generating and manufacturing are large-scale operations, which require major investments in time and money to make changes even when the changes are required or have a cost advantage.

Spinning up and adding capacities in all of these industries, plus the creation of more innovative technologies, will dramatically improve our economy and create a healthy view of our future. What it will do for the overall population and our cultural longevity will be the subject of years of study.

In the end, it is likely that these events will be shown historically to be a turning point in our understanding and acceptance that we as a nation must become energy self-sufficient; we must learn, again, to fend for ourselves, and then to allow others to do the same. These are clear requirements if we are to become the world leader and powerhouse to the rest of the world that we symbolically represented during the past several centuries.

This is, of course, just the start if we are to become responsible stewards for our future. We cannot again create a scenario where we exhaust, or make prohibitively expensive, one source of energy without a plan to offset that source and/or bring a new one online. That plan and the required programs to provide the lifeblood of our economy, energy, cannot be left to chance, the extortion of our enemies, or fate.

We are better than that and have the recorded history to prove it. We are standing on the shoulders of the historic innovators and leaders of our past. We need to emulate their independence, strength, and stamina. We owe it to our heritage and, more importantly, to our coming generations.

The Lesson

Energy is the actual currency for our economy, and most likely, it has been the primary currency for centuries. Understanding this principle helps to motivate the population and to instill pride in being independent and responsible for our own social decisions, using that abundant supply of inexpensive energy.

If we are to continue to advance our cultural and social order, it will come from our understanding and proper use of the energy resources that we have at our fingertips. It will also come from the innovative uses of that energy and the leadership that will be needed to cultivate and direct that use. Finally, it will be furthered with the creation of the next breakthrough energy source that we will inevitably need in the future.

It is time for the general population of this nation to become invested in the innovative process we have demonstrated in the past and can as easily repeat in the near future. For those of you looking for a new career path or just starting your career, the most likely success stories will come from the energy sector and any innovation that uses that energy or makes its use more acceptable, efficient, and affordable.

The time is now, and you are each in a position at this point in history to make a considerable contribution to the life we have all enjoyed the fruits of during our time here.

The Missing Link

If failure is closing in on your heels, then
You are not moving forward fast enough.
Direction and rate may reflect progress,
But your intention chooses the outcome.

The Discussion

Sometime during my earlier years, I heard a joke that stayed with me. Since I seldom remember jokes once I hear them, the longevity of this one must have taught me something of value back then. It was not particularly funny; rather, it was somewhat profound to me at the time. I should note that over the years, I have gleamed at least some of the value out of this remembered joke, and thus, I provide it here for your appreciation.

Picture a man walking down the middle of a street dragging a long chain. He is highly intoxicated, and his movement is rather erratic but pretty much along the center line of the street. The loosely linked chain is following his gait precisely with the links bouncing around due to the roughness of the pavement, but always under the control of the links they are attached, both in front and behind. A police officer passing by in his squad car stops to investigate the situation. On approaching the individual, the officer says, "Why are you pulling a chain down this street?"

The man slowly replied, "Have you ever tried to push one?"

The Lesson

People are often likened to the links in a chain. They have their own energy and tend to move around a lot, but ultimately, if a goal is to be achieved, that link will line up with the others of similar bent to move the mission forward. The noteworthy part of the joke was the dragging versus the pushing. Without proper leadership providing the direction and goals, the links will effectively remain in a loose pile.

As humans, we are effectively, but loosely, linked to each other. We can move around and decide to go in a variety of directions within the constraints of being linked to all other human beings. What helps make us so successful is our ability to establish a goal and with the right leadership form up into a formidable force to get something completed. A chain is a terrible tool for pushing, but when led properly, it is unrelenting in its ability to pull us to where we need to go.

Is There Anything New?

You are the future,
What are you waiting for?

Personal Experience

It is easy to get excited when you are working in a new problem area, which has some special interest to you. For this discussion, I am using the word problem to cover a host of concepts such as a work-related technical problem to ones related to maintenance problems around the house and including taking on a new activity such as a hobby.

As your knowledge increases on the subject at hand, it will naturally become, in most cases even more exciting, especially if you are trying to solve a persistent problem that really needs a clever solution. Initially, what comes from this excitement are the questions of why the topic wasn't investigated before and then how the problem developed in the first place.

What follows this burst of initial excitement is the realization that all of your grand ideas and problem solutions have most likely already been tried and are of public record. At this point, it is the true investigator who doesn't just give up. They continue to push the discovery envelop until they have exhausted all the many additional possibilities that may or may not have already been tried.

Sometimes these investigators come up with a breakthrough for the problem or discover the solution to an unrelated problem that they can apply a new solution to. This is the nature of this investigative beast that has been built into each of us and the one we, and the people around us, have to contend with and suffer through.

As one of our many survival skills this one provides us with the focus and tenacity to get the problem solved or at least make a valiant effort toward the solution. In most cases once, we have been personally hooked into solving a particular problem, no matter what the outcome might be or how stubborn we really become, we will run the beast to ground or resolve that we can't find a workable solution. Note that I have seen some of the best problem solvers come up against a wall to then have them find a solution later after their brains have had a chance to ponder the information without the stress of a timeline or a notion that the problem needs fixing on a personal time schedule. These thoughts are thus the subject of this lesson.

The Discussion

It is said that "There is nothing new under the sun." This is a commonly used saying that comes from the Book of Ecclesiastes in the Old Testament and one that is used quite frequently to cover a variety of topic areas. I suspect it is a rough translation of a more complex thought, but for this lesson, the common saying will suffice. The saying often seems very true especially when working with advanced technology or advanced scientific principles.

As an example, a problem is recognized, a creative solution is prepared, and then the same concept can be found on one or more of the many archival publication sites. This is also true for patent art where a uniquely brilliant insight is soon found covered by one or more patents, either domestic or foreign.

This, on the surface, appears to validate the above adage that there is nothing new under the sun. Unfortunately, this also often provides another reason for organizations to stop their focus on innovation. In other words, why waste time and money trying to solve problems that most likely have already been solved. Innovation can be a very expensive proposition for most companies, particularly so when the outcome is unsure and unclear, and the time and resource requirements are often undefinable.

Of course, when performed properly, these activities can produce trade secrets, patents, and a host of products and commercial opportunities. This, of course, all becomes another expensive part of the commercialization process and unless the product makes it to market this discovery process is but a drain on the bottom line of an organization.

The commercial value comes once the idea is taken to market, the other end of the process, which is often another of the stumbling blocks for some companies. It is easier to focus on what has worked in the past to provide value to the bottom line of the quarterly finances, and often it is very uncomfortable to consider what might work better in the future. It is the word *might* in the last sentence that creates unease with most managers, the leadership, and the board of directors who are always conscious of their uneasy and demanding stockholders.

What can then follow from this fear to commit to innovation is a lack of focus on innovation and a move to downsize or sometimes eliminate their research and development centers, a trend that could become disastrous if there was a wholesale implementation of this trend around the globe.

It turns out that reality doesn't support the saying at the top of this chapter. Even with the millions of existing patents worldwide, the growth rate of patent art is continuing to rise. Plus, while it is more expensive today to support research and development and to then publish the same, the number of published referred articles worldwide is also on the rise.

This would support that there is a continuing growth in new art, admittedly small in percentage to the total in the open literature but sufficient to drive innovation forward and to provide commercial value to the shareholders and valuable products and services to the consumer.

So where are the inconsistencies and contradictions in this saying? It is clear that several companies have cut back their in-house research and development efforts, but some of that work has since been sent out to contract development centers and/or university-based research centers.

Shopping around for better and more efficient solutions by outsourcing or simply releasing undeveloped ideas and technologies to those with specialized talents is often more cost effective, plus it eliminates the need to sustain in-house infrastructure (bricks and mortar).

Focusing on the new ideas while letting others perform the development processes can make good business sense especially for those companies that specialize in production and not product development.

This focus on specialization, knowing what you are good at and staying that course, plus the release of new technology not in your wheelhouse, has created a growth spike in new business start-ups. This is particularly the case in the advanced technology fields, which will in the future provide a bolstering of the nation's overall research and development efforts, not to mention the learning curve advances it provides to the next generation work force.

While these new start-up companies and their related development efforts are often on a smaller scale from the companies they obtained the technology from, their efforts often provide a future source for partnerships, mergers, and/or acquisitions with other small entities or much larger enterprises.

A spirit of focused innovation with a strong view to future prosperity is a key to any nation's or region's ability to gain and then remain a world technology leader. To do this will require an even more intense commitment to research and development (R&D) along with the creation of cooperative environments and agreements between willing partners and even competitors.

It will also require an understanding of the interplay that needs to develop between research and development centers that are nationally and academically based and those that are supported commercially. Maybe even more important are cooperative involvements that need to be encouraged with fledging start-up efforts that often involve basement and home garage laboratories and testing facilities.

Numerous cooperative efforts have already started to appear in direct opposition to the notion that diverse entities cannot work together. It turns out that most of the individuals who preach that we cannot cooperate on R&D efforts using elements of government, industry, and academia are the very ones that hinder the activity.

The imposed, and often supposed, rules that keep these groups apart are buried in the minutia of overdeveloped bureaucracies, an overzealous legal system, and the comfort that comes from doing things the way we have always done them in the past, which most likely stopped working years or decades ago. We are all very good at creating new rules and regulations and not so good at changing or getting rid of them when their useful life has come to an end.

The other problems come from the notion that someone else will handle or take care of the problems. For any of this to work, industry will find the solution, academia will train the next captain of industry or invent the next disruptive technology or, of course, the government will recognize, solve, and fund the needed research and development efforts so we don't have to worry about a thing. How has that been working for us lately, or has it ever really worked? As in the past if it is going to get done, we are going to have to do it, that means us.

Overall, these notions of any kind of a panacea are at best nearsighted and, at worst, delusional. It is true that these government supported R&D centers, along with the academically supported ones, are great storehouses of intellectual capital and physical resources but their ability to react to the needs of their commercial counterparts (the people that make and then take things to market) has been, at best, dismal.

These government supported efforts still fail, and the failure rate appears to be going up. To reduce this failure rate would require us to preplan our measurables, require deliverables and on the subject of accountability, well, that is often nonexistent; thus, we must use the pressures of success that are part of the free-enterprise process. To help us be successful, no for-profit-based company could operate without these requirements, and so most companies stay away from relationships involving government and universities.

More important, publicly and privately supported R&D centers' ability to be farsighted and visionary has often missed the mark. We have numerous government-supported R&D centers around the nation. We have an even greater number of academically based centers supported both publicly and privately. While it is obvious in most cases that there is significant value in the expertise and facilities that they represent and the services they provide, it is also equally non-obvious how to quantify the actual value received as you would for the same investment in a commercial setting.

The Lesson

So is there anything new under the sun? Probably not a lot as far as the basic building blocks go. It is the way it is all put together that constitutes the game changing breakthroughs, as has been the case throughout history. As an example, the notes in a chord or the words on a piece of paper are normally all the same words and notes used by everybody. It is how they are put together that creates the innovation, and if you think about it, you are watching innovation in action every time you read a book, watch a movie, or listen to a new tune. The same principles apply in science and the development of new technology.

Even with all of the naysayers and the created roadblocks that are all around us, the small amount of innovation that does surface, or sneak through, is often all that is needed to guarantee our future, economic prosperity as it always has. What we need is a little more focus and a lot more willingness to cooperate from the very groups we have entrusted to look after our well-being.

For those who argue that it has already been invented or studied or written and produced, you have missed out on one of the most important attributes of our species—a hopeful view of the future, along with the ability to create the innovations that will get us there. As I have often said in the past, if you can't or won't help then at least get out of the way.

What Are They against This Time?

> If there are truly any coincidences in the universe, they are but a coincidence.

The Discussion

For the life of me, I cannot figure out why there is always someone—who with the assistance and participation of others, develops into an organized group or, if so empowered, into a movement—that is opposed to whatever is proposed or suggested. Seriously, there seems to be an opposition quota requirement for every proposal made irrespective of the merit or the value of the original plan, program, or statement.

It is understood that opposing viewpoints are critical to any reasonable decision-making process, but sometimes, the counterpoints have little or no basis in fact or science, relying only on emotional arguments that often have little or no basis in reality. While life lived as a fantasy may be acceptable for some, it does little to promote a healthy social and economic climate for the rest of us who are trying, as best we can, to advance the same.

Clearly, we could try to engage one of the social scientists or psychologists to explain this phenomenon. Maybe if we understood the reward mechanism that drives the opposition, we might be in a better position to at least understand their presence, or better, we might even be able to mitigate their impact before it becomes a costly and time-consuming production. There must be something driving these people, which may have little to do with exercising the gray matter between their ears.

It often appears that the opposing view is simply the flavor of the month, and after the issue is put to rest for a host of reasonably well-thought-out reasons, these same individuals who created the objection deny their original involvement or find some other reason they were so adamant about the issue in the first place.

Maybe, most likely, their emotions take over long before their brain becomes engaged. Maybe it has to do with feelings instead of rational thought. Sometimes their excuse is because they are too stressed and overworked in their daily lives and so the immediate emotional reaction was all that they could muster; plus, they were already upset about something else, and this was a good place to focus their energies. For some, there is the need to be heard, and thus, they feel entitled to do some stumping, no matter what it costs or the damage it creates downstream.

Since there is little enforceable accountability for these opposing views, their actual argument might be, "Why not have a little fun? Enjoy a moment in the spotlight, or possibly just gain a sense of control over a piece of everyone's destiny." Think what would happen if there was a direct financial charge to the participants for all of these unsupportable activities instead of the current everyone-pays doctrine.

No advocate would subscribe to this penalty since without the counterpoints little good would occur, or at least it would be more costly than it is today. Note, of course, that most unsupportable arguments are representative of the opinions of only a small percentage of the involved citizens. Unfortunately, it is the noisy minority that often gets the attention and the rest of the majority simple acquiesces to the barrage, or at times tries to enjoy the spectacle if there is the time and resources to waste.

The question should be, where are the rest of the populace during these objections and debates? The silent majority is getting run over, and worse, they pay for it in higher product and energy prices plus increasing taxes. Maybe when the issue is finally settled, those that knew better should also be penalized for not speaking up like the ones with the private or unsupportable agendas. Of course, that is, again, the current everyone-pays process. Remember, this can be likened to the old taxation-without-representation concept that was one of the key catalysts that created this country. I think we are, or should be, better than this.

Let's face it, we have very little control over our lives at work. And heaven knows we have little or no control at home with our spouses, and if we have teenagers…well you get the picture. What concerns me the most is that perfectly reasonable people, who get the wrong or misdirected information, are willing to commit a wealth of emotional capital, notwithstanding the actual monetary expenses they will have to incur, all without looking at the issues for accuracy. Somehow the emotional plea trumps all commonsense arguments. So what is the solution?

Possible Solutions

Instead of finding a rational way to put these irrational arguments to rest, I think it would be a lot more fun (tongue in cheek) to simply oppose the opposition. That way, we can scream just as loud but use the facts to make ourselves feel better and clearly become superior to those ne'er-do-wells who are clueless and act like fools.

Oh, I guess that would put both sides of the argument effectively in the same boat, where both sides can rail on the other with no hope for a cessation until the audience stops listening or the financial well-being of the parties simply run dry. Clearly, there must be a better way that allows for a counterpoint without the emotions, all based on the best and most verifiable evidence.

The difference in a possibly better plan, instead of falling into the trap of considering only the emotional side of the equation, would be to simply consider the tools used by most scientists and engineers to present the well-documented and corroborated facts. Unfortunately, that route has been tried at times, but for whatever the reason, some of which are referenced above, the facts are simply ignored for the sake of being right and emotionally vested in the intended outcome.

Some people simply want to believe what they want or what they have been told, independent of the facts. Some create their own truth to fit the reality they want to have, and facts are not a part of the issues. For example, several concerned citizens, groups, and organizations condemn coal and demand the closure of coal-fired power plants because they are dirty, dangerous to operate, and they think we should try to set a better example for the rest of the globe. So we are closing coal-fired power plants when the rest of the globe is building them at record rates, and theirs will most likely be much dirtier than what we design and build.

It is no longer a "them versus us" argument; we all breathe the same air and drink the same water. The globe is spherical and what everyone does where they live and work affects all of us, in time. This is completely independent of the myopic view that we are the center of the universe and what happens here stays here.

Modern US-designed coal-fired power plants are cleaner than any other competitor out there. Instead of upgrading the older plants, our solution is to simply close them. Energy production is the key ingredient to a modern and successful society. Coal has been and will continue to be a key element for that energy production, even if not in the US.

Of course, this is all okay because natural gas has finally been rediscovered in the US and that will make up the lost capacities from the coal plant closures. This statement actually has little basis in fact either. If we decide to shut all of our coal-fired powerplants, the next couple of cold winters could show that reality can be harsh and cruel, especially if the needed capacity has not been brought online to compensate for the closures due to coal. When people start suffering and dying from lack of power, the current opposition will most likely switch sides and deny ever having anything to do with this original foolhardy notion.

Losing sight of the forest for the trees becomes an appropriate but often-ignored adage. Consider the overall picture of phasing out one energy resource in favor of another in a safe and affordable fashion. Economics usually does force the better path unless we simply want to look at only a subset of the problems associated with the situation. What happened to leadership that can put the overall program together so people can support and defend our best interests?

Oh, in case you hadn't noticed, we now have naysayers opposing the construction of new natural gas pipelines, which are to feed those new power plants that have yet to be built or are under construction. Businesses operate to minimize costs and maximize profits. They schedule their expansion activities on a tight schedule and any delays can be costly, which we, the consumers, will ultimately have to pay for.

Of course, there is also the continued opposition to the drilling and hydro-fracturing processes, again independent of the proven statistics, all causing us delays in social and economic productivity. These same individuals who believe pipelines are unsafe have never considered what liabilities are created when the same fuel is transported over the road or by rail or ship. This is also independent of the cost savings and improved efficiency of a permanent infrastructure fuel transportation system.

Clearly, these are only a few of the examples of the programs and their opposing forces that we could discuss. The question is what can we do to take advantage of the time and energy of the people who feel compelled to act as an opposing constituency, so that they can contribute in a way that is beneficial to all of us?

Developed Social Orders

We as a country operate as a very diverse and complex social order. This country has gotten old enough to create multiple layers of bureaucracy, none of which have been filtered and corrected for the needs of the present time period. Additionally, our older companies and our social programs, for that matter, are in much the same shape. There is no way to back up to correct what is here, plus, trying to update what was decided in the past is a hopeless task.

The solution is to accelerate the social progress and the technological base from which we have derived our country's authority and just stop looking back at the created problems of the past. The trick is to get ahead of the curve, and instead of our social and government organizations feeding on a stagnant view of the past, the future growth will compel them to look with us to the future.

Unfortunately, to get to this point will require a concerted effort by the population to get on the same page, reduce the typical emotional response, and to take a responsible look at the bigger picture. It will require that we become informed and cognizant of the impact that we have when we unite with a common front.

The interesting part is that we have done these types of movements numerous times in our past. More importantly, not all were associated with going to war or to the moon. Maybe we need another type of battle cry directed at the dissemination of correct information, the mitigation of the irrational emotional response, and an unwillingness to continue to support the art of stupid!

The Story

This lesson started with a detailed discussion prior to telling the relevant story. There was (is) in fact a reason for this approach. I have been guilty, particularly in my younger years, of becoming emotionally vested in efforts and movements that clearly could not be supported by the facts of the day, if I had taken the time to use my brain and hadn't been too busy to dig out the relevant facts. Being busy was, and is, no excuse so let it be said that the most likely reason for my failure to find out what I really needed to know, was (is) laziness.

I tell this part of the lesson here as part of the admissions I often make to ensure that others might learn from my folly. I also never want to forget how easy it is to get involved with emotions without first finding out and understanding the facts behind the issues, so this lesson also serves as my constant daily reminder. Note that at times, I have had to go back and publicly admit to my earlier emotional decisions and then to explain that I now recant those choices.

Several of the environmental issues, not all, that I supported in my earlier years have been shown to be incorrect. I also supported the use of some alternate fuels and energy generation technologies that I have since scientifically proven were not only wrong but would have caused more damage to the environment, the economy, and to us personally, than the then current processes and technologies. Clearly, most any dated technology can be improved upon and so this discussion is for the then current situation and not some future improvements that I would hope we will all look to implement.

It goes without saying that we all are susceptible to a well-prepared emotional pitch. It is for us individually and as a population generally to demand the facts, the proof of those facts, and the accountability of the proposed solution. In other words, we need to be responsible for our own emotions and help keep them balanced with an appropriate number of supportable facts. It is easy for me to say this now, although I probably wouldn't have appreciated this discussion when I was younger and much less inclined to listen to the facts

The Lesson

The right of opposing viewpoints is a necessary requirement in a democratically run organization, and one of the best ways to find the deficiencies in a project or proposal. Unfortunately, if the opposing view is the one with deficiencies, and they are in position to be heard without question or are unopposed then we are all the less for the activity.

What's needed is a voice of reason supported by the complete facts and not the emotions of the moment. Sometimes, the best decisions are painful but necessary and emotions need to be considered as a way to mitigate the impact, but the decision needs to move forward, nevertheless.

These are often hard lessons to learn. We are emotional creatures, and sometimes, these same emotions can blind us to the facts and the needs of the many around us. It is easy to yield to a specific direction, especially if it satisfies our good will or our particular needs. The facts, when properly presented, normally expose our emotional prejudices and, more importantly, our potential conflicts of interest in the final outcome. Find and stay in support of the facts and the emotions of the moment will have less of a personal and professional impact.

It's Not What You Don't Know

No one knows enough to be a pessimist.
—Wayne W. Dyer

The Discussion

There is a lot of language spent on old sayings, adages, and proverbs that actually often make sense and can provide at least a sense of relief when they are encountered or when someone uses them to illustrate an issue at hand. "A bird in hand is worth two in the bush," "Don't trade daylight for dark," and "Don't send ducks to eagle school" are examples of frequently cited sayings each of which should be clear in their meanings "Nice guys finish last," "The light that burns twice as bright burns half as long," and "Early to bed, early to rise, makes a man healthy, wealthy, and wise" are additional examples of the types of sayings that can frequent our conversations.

Each of these sayings will most likely not need explanation since when used the listener can quickly identify with the use. What is most interesting is that these sayings, which are normally clear in their meanings and applications, often have other meanings from earlier times or from different cultures. While this realization may not seem important, the misunderstanding of the meaning of an adage can have a profound impact if used where the meaning is unclear to the recipients who may be working from an entirely different perspective. This is particularly true when different cultures might see, or use, the saying.

For example, the first saying, "A bird in hand is worth two in the bush" seems clear in its meaning saying what you are holding is better than the two you haven't caught yet. Actually, the original saying dates back to medieval falconry where a bird in the hand (the falcon) was a valuable asset and certainly worth more than two in the bush (the prey). Clearly the meanings may be uniquely different in time and place, but they still seem to cover the same basic ideas. This is the nature and the power of old sayings, adages, and proverbs. They seem to find a place in any language and in every culture. If it worked in the past someone will find a way to tweak it to fit today's situations. Here is a classic saying that has been around for well over a century: "It ain't what you don't know that gets you into trouble. It's what you know for sure that just ain't so" (Anonymous).

This saying, in many forms, has been attributed to Mark Twain, Josh Billings, Artemus Ward, Kin Hubbard, and Will Rogers. Since there apparently is no original authorship that can be attributed to any of these individuals the saying is often given an anonymous designation, although these authors each, plus others, used it in their speeches and writings with their own personalized scripting. This is frequently the way old sayings appear and keep reappearing. They are someone's comment taken to heart and often modified during its many future uses to fit any new but similar situation.

The Story

It turns out that this saying has always had significance to me personally. Interestingly, it's only the first part that got my attention that seemed, at least to me, to point to another singular interpretation. It is noted that the entire saying has a clear meaning since we are often guilty of thinking we know something, or letting our emotions rule our thoughts, and then trying to convince others of our firmly held beliefs. These beliefs are located in the knows-for-sure categories, and they can be difficult to counter since the person postulating the idea believes what they are saying independent even of the facts.

Clearly, this quote stands on its own requiring both sentences to convey the original thought. Consider for this lesson only the first sentence of this quote. Taken by itself the sentence begs the reader to accept that it's what you don't know that will get you in the end. This thought has always troubled me since if you know you don't know something, then obviously you need to learn that something. As a result, I posted the following quote on the wall in my office and often in my classrooms. I wish I could identify the author, plus it could even be me, but somewhere in the past, I lost the original memories of who was the creator of this adage. This version of the saying goes: "It's not what you don't know but rather what you don't know that you don't know that will get you in the end."

As I stated earlier, if you know that you don't know something, then it is your choice and responsibility to alter that situation. Unfortunately, if you don't know what that something might be, it is like having someone sneaking up on you to scare you. Knowing that the game of scare is afoot, even not knowing the if, where, and when it might occur is completely different from not knowing that someone might be sneaking up on you.

The Lesson

We, as individuals, seem to be very content in knowing what we know and even in knowing about what we might not know. We most likely make constant decisions in what we want to learn about or have the inkling to discover. The information is out there, and we simply need to decide what we want to learn and what we will leave to others to fill their brains with.

What we all should be concerned about is the information that we haven't realized even exits and how it might ultimately impact all of us. The first step in this process is to acknowledge that we don't know it all, even collectively. In fact, in the scheme of things we most likely don't understand the proverbial drop in the bucket worth of the information this universe has to offer us. All of this information fitting both the good and the bad categories is out there sneaking up on us. I do hope there are many among us looking for that surprise before we all get shocked out of our wits. Remember, "It's not what you don't know but rather what you don't know that you don't know that will get you in the end."

22
Innovation: Will You See It

You don't have to be a world-class player to be a great coach, but you do need to have mastered the fundamentals of the game.

The Issue

Much like the many identified verbal and physical assaults on our social fabric or our collective sensibilities, seeing these issues isn't necessarily sufficient to knowing, understanding, or defining them, especially if personal opinion is the gauge and not some clearly definable metric that everyone can agree on. This needed metric often appears to be as elusive as a proper definition and description of the assault; at least, that is what we keep getting told.

We are advised that our social fabric has been stressed by some word, deed, or ongoing action, and we are to find a way to stop that whatever, and then to mitigate the impact. As in the first paragraph, the needed requirements should involve an exact definition or description of the transgression, the action or plan to remediate the situation, and the metrics put in place to show the efficacy of the fix. This would seem to be reasonable if we are to rally behind fixing the purported problem as a supportive population. The same issues apply to almost everything we try to deal with as a diverse population and one in particular is the concept of innovation.

The Discussion

In every newspaper, magazine and on the lips of almost every political leader, not to mention the gaggle of self-anointed innovation experts, comes the recently discovered reality that the US has fallen behind in the innovation arena. Again, this realization is open to an opposing opinion along with the need to clearly define the wording of the definition of innovation. More importantly, the metrics we are using today as the gauge have most likely changed from the last time we tried to measure this attribute, assuming we could even have properly defined it back then. Back to the first paragraph and that elusive definition.

It is time to wake up. The fact that we have fallen behind is old news, and for those of us who matured in the last century, we know where we have been, and we are currently not up to any standard that was set in the past century. We also haven't yet identified just how far behind we have fallen, not just from the numerous foreign economies we trade with, but also from the dizzying height we used to view the rest of the world from. Yes, it has only been two to four generations ago that not only were we at the top of the list, on most any economic and personal indicator-of-value measurement, we were also so far ahead of the pack, it wasn't worth looking back.

So what was so different back then and what caused the decline? Some say it all started with a sense of complacency resulting from a feeling of supremacy, probably with a little bit, or a lot, of national arrogance. Others say it all started with the steady increases in taxation, the proceeds of which were being used for growing numbers of programs that only managed to level the playing field instead of raising the bar in the demand for continued and growing excellence.

Some say it is from the clamor over the ever-increasing number of rules, regulations, policies, and don't forget, penalties that is putting a stranglehold on the free-market system that made this country the history-making, economic powerhouse that the world used to envy and look up to.

It could also have resulted from the large number of multinational mega-companies that some even say control the desires and choices of the consumer in this country. What you get from all of this aren't just disincentives for starting a business, it additionally creates levels of overhead that reduces and often removes any competitive advantage innovation might provide, at least for some.

Maybe it could also be a sense of entitlement that seems to be gaining a foothold in our society. The notion of working hard and being responsible for what you do and then receive seems to have lost its way and gone over to the what's-in-it-for-me-now syndrome.

Coupled with this, there seems to be the notion that someone else is always responsible for the decisions being made, including the ones the individual makes themselves. This tends to fly in the face of any reality that makes sense to me since poking a sleeping bear will most likely have an immediate, and, most likely, permanent impact on my well-being. Yet people believe there shouldn't be consequences for decisions made or actions taken, including the stupid ones.

So what is the answer and which one of these issues is it? Surprisingly, it is a combination of all of them, in varying degrees, and at the same time, none of these. While contributory, and yes, each of these issues needs to be addressed if we are to again have sustainable and long-term growth, they all pale in comparison to the real villain, that of thinking instead of knowing what innovation is. Not understanding the real problem, in this case, the definition means we continue to treat the resulting symptoms. So we are back to that concept called innovation and its definition, again.

Innovation is not just a word to describe the next best electronic gadget or process, it is a philosophy of action, belief, and understanding. It is a way to function not only for the inventor or visionary decision-maker, it is an expectation for everyone in, or influenced by, the process of innovation.

It is that state of mind where with each new improvement and change, there is an accompanied moment of surprise, quickly followed by what needs to happen to get on board and why did it take so long in coming, once it is in place.

At almost every level of management and leadership throughout this country, and in most of the other older industrialized countries, there is a predominance of often highly-qualified, competent, and well-intentioned people who understand the need for innovation, but at the same time, often wouldn't know it even if it was given to them in a nicely wrapped package. Even these individuals are receptive to innovation once it is revealed, even if it is disruptive to their current station in life and business, but they then often provide little value in getting it up and running and to the marketplace.

As is often the case, everyone in those decision-making positions is already overworked. They are well versed and trained in what they need to do to continue the successful completion of their assignments. They are trained to look for and correct any flaws or changes in the activities they are responsible for, all the while they know or have been told that they need that next big innovation to get to the next profitability level. This, of course, they want without any personal risk and only if it doesn't interfere with their current job assignments that they already have too many of on their plate.

For those of you who really know what innovation is, this is quite comical. Innovation by its very nature is change (often major), risky, uncomfortable, and often disruptive of the status quo. They are the very things that current managers are hired and trained to avoid, and often get fired for if they fail to address. Remember, we often celebrate as visionaries and gamechangers in their death, the very people we condemned and prosecuted during their lifetimes.

It is the innovators that will make the dramatic changes and who will steer us to a new financial and motivational heading in the future. We still need the great managers and leaders to continue to drive the current and hopefully improving economy until those changes take hold. We will then need them to run those new efforts, to free up our innovators to do what they do best: see a problem or opportunity and provide the visionary response.

Note that these current managers and leaders are effectively part of the problem and not the solution. They, like so many of our decision makers, think they know what innovation is. The reality of that error is all around us. Those that know, the true innovators, are not currently in positions of authority and most likely will not be until they create their own business enterprise.

Some of you may say this is clearly wrong; that with a little time and a lot of money, we can build a program to train this next generation of innovators from the current ranks of successful managers and leaders. All I will say is that you haven't studied history well enough, for most of the great men and women that created our industrial machine, yielding the standard of living we all enjoy, did not come from the well-established businesses of the day.

They were clearly not referred to as normal, patient, cooperative, and the list goes on, and by the way, they weren't trainable or conformists. They were born to or soon acquired the innovative bent and while everyone in our free-market culture has at least a smidgen of that same innovative spirit, a true innovative revolution using all these shared talents will not come until those next-generation of historic figures comes forward to do their thing.

If you want to know what's holding them back, just look at the differences in today's business environment in contrast to the climate of fifty to one hundred years ago. As mentioned before, these innovators must now contend with a staggering set of rules and regulations, don't forget the penalties, all adding to the overhead and stalling the introduction of anything new and forbid that their ideas should be controversial, or a gamechanger. While change is inevitable, with it comes opposition from a myriad of organized groups, and from the media, even when there is little or no connection of these groups to the real issues.

The current tax structure is mind-numbing, plus big business has become an efficient machine, and as such, it knows how to handle competition, or threats, to their product and business structures. They also know how to navigate through the myriad of problems from governing bodies and often hide these interferences under a cost of doing business philosophy. They assume that these same constraints will work more against their competition and thus give them an edge, especially the smaller competitors. While the big financial prize for innovation is still out there, it is harder to find and even harder to keep than it was in the not-so-distant past.

What might surprise you is that even with these additional constraints, much of which we should address to help us again become a world competitor, I believe the innovation revolution has already started. I see this visionary drive in the young people that I have had the privilege to work with. I hear it in the language they use and the vision of the future they expect to create.

The Lesson

Simply put, innovation's time has come as it did in the past, and while the often-mindless rhetoric for defining innovation is strong, with the associated myriad of meaningless and expensive programs being vetted, even those programs won't stop the change. The real concern, if we continue with business as usual, is that the innovation process will be slowed or, what I would consider as a real travesty, these next generation innovators will find a more conducive environment to work in somewhere else.

What I believe these innovators have discovered, and what we have been slow to realize, is that in the game we call "us" or "them," there never was a "them." We are it, and even with all of the contrived evidence to the contrary, we are responsible for what we do and have, and it is time to grow up as a nation and take responsibility for what we have or haven't done in the past to clear the path to the future. These young people are willing and capable to affect a change. Trying to placate or restrict them will only increase their resolve and their mobility.

I also think they will have the opportunity to exercise the free-market opportunities this country was founded on and will with stubborn, visionary effort receive those awards, as was prevalent in the past. All we need to do, at a minimum, is get out of their way and if we are responsible enough, remove some of the obstacles in the above list to help them get a quicker foothold. They really are remarkable, if viewed from my vantage point.

23

Changing Cycles

> There are risks and costs associated to a program
> of action. But they are far less than the long-range
> risks and costs of comfortable inaction.
> —John F. Kennedy

The Discussion

There are a great number of naturally occurring cycles, or rhythms, which we often observe, sometimes identify with, or in numerous cases just plain ignore. The most obvious cycle comes with birth and ends with death, the cycle of life, which governs most everything we do, consciously and often subconsciously. Clearly, it is one cycle we simply can't ignore although as we get older, we try to diminish or cover up the outward signs.

It is interesting to observe that when we are younger, we try to look older, and well, you know what happens as we get older. Clearly, the aging process is a natural cycle that all living creatures tend to live with. So why is it that we don't just enjoy each part of the cycle to its fullest extent instead of enviously looking ahead or, during our later years, looking back? Each moment in time is a treasure for our use and that is why it is called the present.

It is noted that those early first years after birth can be somewhat trying, but then we move into those comforting, and hopefully healthy, midlife years, which wishfully could go on forever except for the telltale signs that seem to keep cropping up when we look in the mirror, no matter what we try to do or ignore.

While scientists may one day learn to extend those more enjoyable and productive years of our lives, the reality is everything is on a finite time scale, one that is neither constant nor predictable. While this is the classic example of a rhythmic cycle for all living creatures there are numerous others such as food tastes, commercial products, the latest fashion, and even scientific postulates and cultural moirés, to name but a few.

It is often said that art imitates life, in whatever definition you may want to attach to art. There are many who contend that this saying often needs to be reversed where life is constantly trying to imitate art. This would suggest that one person's fantasy or futuristic view becomes the crucible for change in the future, at least for their personal change.

These are the changes that will inevitably occur even though prior to that time the idea had not been conceived or possibly was believed to be a violation of certain physical or scientific principles. Maybe the real explanation is that art and life go hand in hand pushing or possibly leap-frogging each other to drive us forward, and possibly away from the brink of disaster.

The evidence that we might be able to alter the naturally occurring cycles or rhythms of the environment, the world, and in the future the universe, are all around us. One person, or a group, describes a process or discovers something new and then almost like magic the world discovers this new art and then, in what is often an explicable process, adopts it.

There are some experts that now contend that the process of learning doesn't just occur through conscious effort as in the classroom or experientially, it also seems to be transmitted generationally or through some as yet-to-be-discovered or defined medium that may exist pervasively around us.

This would indicate, and there is ample evidence to support the notion, that the world that we have helped to develop will continue to evolve and be defined by the art that we all continually create, intentionally, unintentionally, or serendipitously. There seems to be no last station on this train track, and thus, we will continue to seek even loftier heights by standing on the shoulders of the great men and women that have preceded us to see, or imagine, what is, or may be, around the next bend. No matter what we want to believe, the way things are, as with any time in history, won't remain that way for long—almost independent of the personal energy we expend to try to keep it that way.

Clearly, in the cosmic scheme of things, you can continue to maintain your set of beliefs, even when there is ample evidence to the contrary, and force your reality on the others willing to accept or subjugate themselves to that belief. In the end, though, you will pass on and others will pick up the more promising thread of the day, yours being lost to antiquity or recorded in the annals of history or as an epitaph on your tombstone.

Those Other Cycles

In the scheme of things, we just don't live long enough to have that large of an impact, or control, over our lives, and as such, we should either humble ourselves to the reality of our meager existence or become ecstatic over the notion that we have managed to exist in this time and location in the first place.

Assuming that we have adequately covered the living creatures' portion of our existence, there are other cycles and rhythms we influence and are impacted by. Much like those personal beliefs and our life span, a similar process cycle applies to products, customer needs, and commercial-industrial/societal relationships. It also impacts the types and styles of food that we consume and the hobbies and activities we participate in.

On top of all of this comes the associated cultural and governmental requirements and regulations, all hopefully meshing together for the good of mankind and the world we live in. What should be abundantly clear is that while our lifecycle has not changed significantly; although we have extended our lifespans, other cycles around us are becoming shorter or briefer, such as the product lifecycle of almost every goods and services we barter for.

What used to be changes in our lives that were generational in scope are now at best only a few years in duration. This means we can now no longer be comfortable with the decisions we made yesterday. Plus, we don't have the luxury of waiting to see the culmination of the change, will it just go away on its own, or how someone else handles a similar situation. Waiting simply adds to the complexity of the situation, and then we end up reacting instead of being proactive.

This is not to say that this evolving and accelerating development process is not fraught with its own set of difficulties, noting that while haste can generate waste, indecision can cause disasters. History has clearly recorded the countless misdirection that we have taken to get to this point in our social and industrial development. History, fortunately, also shows us the great changes that helped direct us to where we currently are—for both the good and the bad. It seems that we are often too quick to look at the historical notation oblivious of the sequence of events that had to have occurred prior to, during, and after the critical event happened to allow it to become noteworthy and a factor in our lives for the present going into the future.

It is notably important to remember and learn from those past events and the people who lived them, but this all pales in importance to what can be learned from the process that caused the event and how we as a species reacted and accommodated the changes that resulted. Discovering the critical factors that created the new art and then the difficulties that had to be endured, or overcome, to implement those changes are the most important parts of the lesson and the one that is often ignored, marginalized, or not clearly understood by the current generation. It is from these lessons that we can learn the most.

Change, particular disruptive change (gamechangers), normally comes at a cost: mostly through the loss of personal comfort and security. It is in this result that most people find leaving things the way they are to be less disconcerting than to embrace the changes that are necessary for a productive future.

Life may begin at the edge of the comfort zone, but familiarity and predictability beg to extend the illusion that life can be made a little more controllable, albeit more boring. Some people simply ignore the reality that change will continue to happen no matter what we choose to believe, often leaving us with long-term problems that could have been handled more easily using a long-term developmental strategy, instead of hiding our heads in the sand or finding solace in the current stock market quotient.

The Lesson

A starting place for what some might call a healthy, visionary strategy could be learned from those that came before us and who suffered through, effectively, the same elements of change that we are also going to be faced with, albeit ours at an accelerating rate. Using this methodology would then reflect and account for the fact that change is always upon us, thus obviating the costs required to maintain things the way they are and the resulting impact that all of this has on our environment and our personal and financial resources. Maybe more important would be the reduction in the discouragement and disillusion that we heap on ourselves and our youth who, by necessity and, as a result of the changes that they embrace surviving their youth, find all a little bit boring and archaic.

In general, we, as adults and the people in positions of authority, the current power brokers if you will, are expected to be the decision-makers for the present and the future. Instead, what we seem to be doing, at least in large part, is maintaining the status quo and ignoring the current problems well into the future. Worse, it appears that we are willing to do this at any cost even when the evidence is in front of us to support the contrary. The irony springs from the obvious better choice that somehow gets overlooked no matter how good the art is.

So why do we continue to make the less than visionary decisions? Why choose the most convenient or safest decisions? Why look to the present for future successes when history tells us that the current solutions become the problems of the future? The answer lies in who and what we are. No matter what we say and do, there is an intrinsic need to take care of ourselves and those closest to us and to allow the presence of as little risk as possible.

In most cases, it will always appear that the current process or world view is the best understood, and it is also the most controllable. Fortunately, in most cases, this process is fairly benign, and with the mix that comes from the many others who are making their own contributions, it all works out in the end, at least it has in the past.

It appears, though, that the present, and soon to be the future, will be coming at us at an accelerating rate. We may not have the luxury of waiting for the mix to heal us along with the problems we create through our very presence.

As Bob Dylan once wrote in one of his lyrics, "Things they are a-changing," and the current decision-making process is not responsive enough to stay abreast of the changing landscape of our futures. As some have done in the past, we will need to rise above our base instincts and start making the difficult decisions that will encourage us to progress and still allow for the protection of the world we live in.

Clearly, the next generation will need to approach problems differently. Why not help by modeling a better way for them to learn from today, or as Heraclitus, the Greek philosopher, once said, "The only constant in life is change." It is us that needs to change by being proactive and not reactive. Time to embrace and effect the change that is coming. It turns out that art and life are part of a constantly changing cycle. We just need to embrace that change to get the most out of the current cycle.

Science and Technology

Science and the resultant advancements in technology are immeasurable, unpredictable, and often unimaginable.

The Discussion

It is hard to think at times how far the human race has come in its social development and its ability to master the environment we live in. We bend the will of Mother Nature to allow us to flourish in harsh environments where a few centuries ago we would have perished. The use of the discoveries in science and technology have opened up a floodgate of opportunities for us to enhance survival and to socially flourish. This has also come at a high price and toll on the environment that we have often taken for granted.

We are not completely irresponsible, though, and the same science and technology used for our survival are used to improve and rehabilitate what we have often taken advantage of in haste, the environment. More importantly, as technology improves and the science of living together as a planet increases, we will improve our working relationship with this world, as if we really have a choice.

It is here where science and technology and the human race will come to a juncture. How we will survive in the future will be entirely dependent on our advances in science and technology and our presence of mind needed to protect the world we have to survive and flourish in.

I have often been asked why we can't just return to earlier times where things were much simpler and the burden on the environment was much less. I suspect the argument would have some merit if we were all willing to massively reduce our living and survival requirements. We would also most likely have to reduce our population by about half and cut out the current expected amenities we have all grown so fond of.

The reality is that the progress train has already left the station, and if you are not on it, you will most likely have a poor existence or not survive at all. Note also that earlier generations most likely were more damaging to the environment per person than we are. There are now just a lot more of us than before.

If we are to get back to the illusive, pristine world we are constantly reminded of, then it will be through science and technology that will allow that process to happen. I am not completely sure what that perfect, pristine world should look like since history shows the planet also has an evolving nature and as such, I am never sure what image we should set as the preferred one.

It turns out that if we weren't here Mother Nature would mosey along doing her thing and providing her long-term remedies to the changes dealt her in changing amounts of solar radiation plus the unexpected volcanoes and meteorites that have plagued her for eons. By the way, she has stumbled along quite successfully and if we should evaporate one day from this planet, I doubt she would even notice our absence.

Of course, we are here, and for our children's sake, I hope we will remain here and, at the same time, become better stewards of the world we call home. I believe it will be through science and technology where we will strike a proper balance with our wonderful home and still allow for the human race to advance and flourish. To this end, I crafted a short poem reflecting these thoughts. I often used it in my classrooms to help stimulate discussions. It is now the lesson for thought from this chapter.

The Lesson

As for Science and Technology

The value of science and the advancements in technology are immeasurable, unpredictable, and often unimaginable. Without them, though, the current global social order and our ability to sustain human life would be, at best, marginal. It is through these crafted capabilities that we will continue to advance mankind in ways that only the philosophers and fiction writers can foretell.

Assuming there are no catastrophic or cataclysmic events on our horizon, it would be fair to assume we will find the solutions to the never-ending problems that we continuously create as a result of solving some previous set of problems. Thus, life will go on, and the social order will advance through the myriad of endless possibilities, most likely perpetuated on the advancements created through science and technology.

The Virtual Commercialization Model

If you have not developed the essence of leadership present within, how can you expect to lead others to needed changes in the future?

The Discussion

We, as a nation, are best when we have a shared vision and feel that we are able to contribute to that cause. This is well-documented in the literature where we have risen up in support of the causes and needs that have developed in our past. With the continuing development in our communications infrastructure, we can be even more responsive to the needs of this nation and even more capable in delivering solutions to the problems of the day.

In a growing number of regions around the country, collaborative professionals are working together to create changes in the social and physical aspects of our culture through the use of their collective, creative intellects. It is with this ability to communicate on a realtime basis that has allowed for this evolution in our ability to respond to a recognized need. These nebulous groups are often focused on a variety of problem topics where each of them has the common goal of producing tangible solutions and/or products that can fix a problem, answer a need, or take advantage of an opportunity.

Most of these organizations are diverse in nature bringing together the needed personnel specific to the current identified effort and they are often working virtually. These groups are often fluid in their memberships and associations where the team that finishes a project may not completely resemble the original founding group, who may have moved on to other efforts.

The participants range from individuals to small organized groups and in many cases larger businesses that can shepherd and support these developmental activities under a common banner. These loosely organized activities can then mainline the products and solutions into the marketplace either using a participant in the original activity or by going outside through a licensing model.

The professionals in these activities are often employed through unrelated companies or are associated with research and development efforts, which are often unrelated in their daytime employment mission to the current effort. They may even be experts or consultants with the extra bandwidth to take on additional work outside of their normal income interests. The common thrust in most of these individuals and associations is to find, fix, solve, and return investment value to the stakeholders who are the participants, and ultimately all of us.

Another characteristic of these working groups is that they are often virtual in their location and sometimes even viral in the way they conduct their research, development, and commercialization activities, and even in how they collaborate. Some of these participating members may never know all of the participants or ever even get a chance to meet them personally or online.

You will find these groups to be made up of experts from the focus areas, representatives from businesses that need the solution or want to establish a new market, or a compilation of professionals that can provide their piece of the puzzle when needed. Some of these professionals even give their talents away just for the chance to participate in something useful or because by themselves they think they have little chance to achieve the final solution.

The bricks and mortar for these activities can be found in home offices and garages, university offices and laboratories, and corporate and national research centers. Most of the work effort is part of the contribution the participants are committing, in addition to the work they do in their day jobs.

Because of the nature of these efforts, the overhead is nearly net-zero since all these facilities are effectively already managed and paid for. The actual expenses come from the direct payment or in-kind donations that are used to facilitate the completion of the effort. The limited direct overhead comes from the visible presence that is sometimes needed when the product and/or process is looking for another solution or contributor or is ready for market.

The outcome of this model is the minimized use of up-front capital matched by multiples of in-kind contributions where the profits from the activities are used to reward the stakeholders proportionally while often holding back increasingly larger amounts of seed capital from the profits for the next round of efforts for commercialization.

Stakeholders can come and go from this effort and/or participate in more than one of the projects during any given time period. The common theme for all these efforts is the problem solution or product creation, which becomes innovation and entrepreneurism at its best. These efforts are motivated by the willingness to take advantage of current and future opportunities and the need to return value to the participating stakeholders. This is clearly a low-hanging fruit model, at least initially, and one that, with the correct focus, can bring products and services, and thus jobs, to market in an expedient and successful manner.

The Lesson

The latest generation is better equipped to take advantage of this virtual commercialization model than previous generations, but the process is becoming effective within all the age groups. The reality is, if you have a willingness to contribute and have a skill or expertise needed for the solution, there is a place for you in this virtual problem-solving environment.

For those of you already participating in these new venues, congratulations and welcome to the future in entrepreneurism. For those who believe this is a little too innovative or that it can't possibly work, remember the lyrics from the Bob Dylan song—"The times they are a-changin'." I hope you will decide to catch up with what's going on all around you, even if it is later.

Too Many Words

Be succinct.

The Discussion

I learned a valuable lesson early in my career that, during the time required to the preparation of progress and final technical reports on funded research and development projects, that has also been proven to have application to a host of responses to everyday questions. As was stated to me by a wise old friend, it takes only a few words to confirm an expected result and a long dialogue to explain the opposite. Think about it: if someone asks you how you are feeling, how the work is coming along, or are we on schedule, if the answer is positive, then as few as one word or even a gesture, such as a nod, will often suffice as an answer.

Since you are thinking about it, consider what happens in most communications when the expected answer is not delivered. Providing a "Not so good" to the "How are you feeling?" will most likely prompt a series of questions that will probably make you feel even worse and cause you regret in having answered truthfully.

The same applies to all forms of communications, and from my vantage point, and for the record, it is always better to be truthful and handle the issuing barrage of questions then to wait and have the truth come out later. This course of action goes along with the negative impact of both the less than positive response added to your propagation of a lie.

When you were a kid the often-asked question was "Did you do your homework?" The yes answer normally got a nod of approval or a good, possibly a great, or a host of other positive affirmations. The no answer, if you remember, resulted in a series of additional questions requiring an equal number of answers from you, some vague excuses and even a misdirection response if you were quick enough to come up with one.

The misdirection might even be the dog ate my homework, which I would have used when I was young, but we didn't have a dog. Also, added to your answers was the continuous stream of excuses, couched as reasons, and promises to do something in exchange for this transgression or oversight at some later opportunity.

Independent of the question, the negative or unexpected response normally results in the need to explain yourself, justify the disappointment, or explain how and why you will do better next time. It turns out that getting older and assuming greater responsibilities means you still have to answer the questions, but the stakes tend to be a little higher and the consequences more severe and, possibly, even permanent.

It turns out the problem is not with the person asking for the answer; it is, in fact, the person providing the answer. If the assignment is clear and reasonable and you have promised an outcome at some designated level of completeness on an agreed to time schedule, then you need to have either the expected answer or know why, have a fix for the situation, and a plan to complete the assignment, hopefully on an acceptable schedule without the need for additional resources.

Noting that everyone makes mistakes once in a while, for some of us all of the time, most reasonable people will allow for a new plan and expected delays. This is normal in most relationships, but I should point out that if you don't have a dog, then you need to find an equally valid excuse for a failure to do homework, chores, or to practice your earlier begged-for band instrument.

For those of you a little further along with your careers, then it is important to always understand all the details of the assignment. A complex problem or assignment will have numerous tasks and subtasks to get to a proper or required solution. If the problem has been laid out properly, then an affinitive answer at each stage will normally allow for short answers. On the not-so-positive responses, the failure on the smaller tasks assignments will keep your personal competencies out of the discussion with the assumption that the end result will come out okay.

Interestingly, the need for elaborate negative reports will not work in the professional fields as it didn't when you were a kid. Professionals can't use the "dog ate my report" even if they have a dog since it is expected that a professional would have made it impossible for the dog to get to the report in the first place. I will point out that as adults, we have a plethora of excuses that we can use to not report positively on something, such as a computer failure, power was off, "Great-grandma had to be taken to the hospital," and the list goes on. The reality is that the professional will plan for as many contingencies as possible and execute the plan accordingly.

The Story

As an example of planning for contingencies, I once led a team to develop a new technology. That team had worked for over a year on the project and had a final report due on a specific date at a specific time. The meeting was in a distant city, and the participants were all out-of-towners, two out of country. All four of my in-house team were to appear at the meeting to help make the presentation. The presentation and the success of the meeting guaranteed another year in program funding, so we knew we had to do a great job. Note the project results were positive, but the individuals providing the funding still wanted a formal presentation, made in person.

To be sure of success we had planned for all the travel contingencies, all four of us carried copies of the final report and the presentation. We had all practiced giving the report so that part was covered. We sent one of our team members to arrive the day before the meeting, and the rest of us secured passage on the best flights to get there with sufficient time to comfortably make the meeting.

Two of our team members didn't arrive, one because of a cancelled flight, the other missed a connecting flight. Two of us made the presentation, which impressed the participants with our planning. Note that three of their group also didn't arrive on time due to similar travel problems, and yes, we received our second year of project funding.

I understand with today's technology those contingencies would not need to be planned for, and most likely, the meeting would have been held virtually, but back then, the personal touch was an expected requirement. Note that while things have changed, everyone still needs to plan for contingencies and eventualities.

The Lesson

The lesson here is that in most all situations, a well-planned activity will result in less words, often making excuses or pointing fingers unnecessary. The requirements attached to a completion schedule needs to be established and made clear to all the participants. Then if there is a problem, such as an unexpected complexity or a need to redirect the efforts, it will be easier to approach the person making the request in contrast to waiting until report time and then being forced to make excuses or retractions. In all cases, it will take far fewer words to provide a preferred positive outcome or a recommendation for a different path to the same or similar outcome.

Practice Activity

Since I learned the lesson well, I often took every opportunity to explain the need to be on top of an effort and to not make excuses. In other words, I asked my fellow participants to find ways to minimize the use of words in providing the requested answer. The following is one of the exercises I asked my students and colleagues alike to try.

Create two-word phrases that clearly describe a possible answer to a question. Note that there were similar exercises that used other than two-word phrases, but this one had the most profound impact. As an example, for the one-word answers the words "stop" or "go" and "yes" or "no" work very effectively, but then, it gets a little harder to find more. I have provided a few of the two-word answers developed by my students for you to consider. With a little practice, you will come up with many more. Plus, the practice will help you in the future prepare the proper, short answer when needed.

1. Deliver promise
2. Require results
3. Deliver value
4. Improve quality
5. Stand fast
6. Stay true
7. Acknowledge praise
8. Perfect enough
9. Never quite
10. Demand respect
11. Make better
12. Expect advancements
13. Be passionate
14. Smile often

27

Stop Doing Stupid

> But the one thing you can't do,
> You just can't fix stupid.
>
> —Ron White

The Discussion

As of the printing of this book, I have now lived for well over seven decades, and during a majority of that time, I have had the honor and privilege to serve in a variety of capacities as teacher, research professor, and at times, as a technical and business mentor. To a lesser extent, I have also served as a business owner and decision-making adviser for several technology start-ups. This mix of experiences is the reason for many of the things that I have accomplished and even more in the specific directions my life has led me.

Sprinkled throughout all those years, particularly in my teaching roles, have been the constant, and actually quite the normal, series of questions associated with student-teacher/mentor interactions. This is the normal learning process that I doubt will change soon, even with all the social media and interactive technology capabilities we are currently developing.

It should be noted that while these new internet teaching possibilities are more aligned with Socratic learning philosophies, when compared to that of the current large lecture-style classroom, it will take some time to validate and develop these capabilities and their potential for enhanced learning.

Either way, in most of these learning environments, there always seems to be the interference and interruptions from the inevitable, and often dreaded, stupid question. Yes, I said it, there are stupid questions no matter what you have been told. For those people who insist that there are no stupid questions, they clearly haven't paid much attention, or they are one of the many sources for these plagues on a person's patience. The questions in these classroom situations, as an example, often have no bearing on the subject at hand, serving at best as a distraction and worse as a divergence.

I will admit that some, maybe a majority, of the myriad of questions that I have received in the classroom are related to my often-unorthodox way of conveying the required information along with its importance. The rest, though, can be chalked up to the inherent failure of the student to fully grasp the new, foreign concept or to connect the appropriate neurons to synergize their next great aha moment.

There might, of course, also arise the occurrence of the desire or need by some participants in the process to derail or stall the learning process. Such motives may spawn from apathy, a sense of being lost, or a concern that the learning differential might be expanded for the more ambitious participants if the current rate of knowledge transfer is not slowed down just a little.

While for me most of these learning peculiarities apply to the classroom-based, student-teacher relationship, they can also apply equally well to all interactions where someone is learning something from someone or something. If there are failures within any of these interactions they can, for the most part, be attributed to inherent differences associated with communication skills, the age of the participants, or possibly the age differential between the conversing parties, as well as the number of participants in the exchange, and the actual or perceived roles of the participants, among the other reasons mentioned above.

As I started to indicate earlier, it is within these questions and the exchange of information, plus the value of such in the handling of life's problems, where the true power of the learning process occurs. I should also add that this is where feelings of satisfaction are experienced when the information transfer is successful and an understanding resonates in both parties, sometimes more so for the instructor.

Unfortunately, it is too often the case that the questions are of little or no value to the subject at hand, and as such, they become a waste of effort and, by any reasonable economic or social measures, a waste of valuable resources like time and money.

Interestingly, this set of conditions and reactions are not only applicable to the educational process, they are inherent characteristics in all communication processes and particularly so in management and leadership scenarios. For these latter cases, it is not just the stupid or foolish question that causes the problems; it is also the actions, statements, strategies, proposals, etc., that occur during these efforts. It should be noted that these could occur amongst all members of the interaction including the leaders and the managers. No one is immune to being stupid.

The Human Story

One of the primary reasons we, as a species, have been so successful, in addition to our opposing thumbs, is our ability to learn and to take advantage of acquired knowledge to make decisions, solve problems, and from these efforts create a stronger economy and a better social order. These capabilities also allow us to aggressively protect ourselves from the varied and changing environment we choose to live in, amidst the diverse personalities that we choose to live around.

It is in the success of that information and knowledge transfer along with the ability to make appropriate decisions that allows us to accelerate that survival process, which has made us so remarkably successful as a species, even if it has put our environment in peril at times.

In other words, it is in our ability to successfully teach, or mentor, what is needed to the next group of participants and to also provide the leadership and management skills that helps to precipitate the next great something that is needed to stay ahead of the problems the earlier generation created by solving their own yesterday's problems.

This seems to be the nature of the beast for any advancing technological society where the notion of simply stepping off the progress merry-go-round in favor of an earlier, simpler time is a train that has long since left the station.

In all these human-based processes, there is the inherent need to learn what needs to be conveyed and to do so in a well-managed environment. This applies as well, if not more so, in organizations large enough to require a management and leadership structure.

Note that it may not be entirely clear that all effective managers and leaders teach effectively. In fact, although the classroom setting may be seldom employed, the mentoring and modeling as well as the instructional aids and directives provided can constitute and illustrate a most effective teaching methodology.

This, of course, assumes that any or all the participants have not fallen prey to the stupid question examples provided above. In this case, though, it isn't just the stupid question that is the culprit; it is the acceptance of stupid as an acceptable operational model that generates the larger problem.

The Story

There is an old adage that reads "the suffering of fools," which for this lesson is the passive form of the "stop doing stupid" in the title of this lesson. In most well-run organizations, there are several individuals who are frequently accused of not suffering fools very well. For the most part, they are welcome additions to these organizations, albeit not so much when you are the subject of their attention and scrutiny.

The story, though, is not as simple as the three words of the title of this lesson or the better-known "suffering of fools." In fact, the need to define the situation goes much deeper than an old adage, although there is often a lot of merit to old sayings since they usually develop from a multitude of predictably annoying occurrences.

In this case, the active form, "stop doing stupid," requires an immediate response and often a call to action, if waste is to be reduced and value is to be added. Note that people who react to stupid questions and actions too quickly and/or too loudly are often placed on the endangered species list, especially if the stupid in question is emanating from their boss. Sometimes, prudence needs to be exercised in these situations or at least expressed in a more socially acceptable manner.

While the inability for this select group to simply stay quiet when things become stupid might be chalked up to an aberrant chromosome or a problematic childhood, it turns out that of all of the possible and often identified annoying human habits this one may have significant long-term social value. Noting that excellence often creates even more excellence, what do you think stupid creates?

It is becoming clear to a growing number of individuals that we as a society have sat far too long letting people, who have perfected the art of acting and saying stupid, continue to add ever-increasing levels of crap to our already busy existences. This can either occur through accident, oversight, ignorance, laziness, or just plain self-entitlement. Actually, the particular reason has little importance. The reality is that stupid foolishness has to be fought at every turn or it will, as it has, start to dominate our lives.

To be fair, a few definitions and explanations are in order. Note that this lesson will define, and not justify, the total failure to get past a clearly foolish or stupid comment, or action, even when one of us might be the willing participant or originator of the same. The rolling of the eyes, the loss of attention, or a change of subject is just never enough of a response for the ever-vigilant and intellectually present participant.

These violations of the commonsense mandate must be dealt with immediately and handled abruptly since Mother Nature, or the Darwin Edict is often hit or miss, or it is too slow to weed out the truly stupid participants and their stupid contentions.

The reference to stupid is not to be confused with ignorance where the uninformed can get a free pass unless the people in question want to stay ignorant because of laziness or as a means to mitigate possible future liabilities. For example, ignorance of the law now seems to represent a probable courtroom plea and, sometimes, even a free pass especially for the more innocent looking.

Eventually, early retirement, or in some few cases termination, can take care of the culprit if repetition is the best teacher, or even better, the Darwin effect may eliminate them and the problem altogether. As for ignorance being bliss, we should have no respect for those individuals who bury their heads in the sand since they know they are not heeding the signs and thus choose to play dumb.

This lesson is also not referring to stupid from an intelligence standpoint. The spectrum of intelligence among humans, like all living creatures, is wide, and we are all equally qualified to "step in it," as the saying goes, no matter where we fall on the intelligence scale.

I suspect the lower end of the intelligence scale is far less guilty of contributing to foolishness or stupid actions because of their lack of reserves, both financially and personally, to cure the consequences, if and when they should occur. So this segment of the intelligence spectrum may, in fact, pay more attention to the world around them and the role they play in it than any other group.

The average to moderately intelligent and possibly the super intelligent are probably the most used to getting away with "stupid" because they often have the financial reserves to cover up their accidental or deliberate oversight. Plus, they most likely have the refined and often-practiced abilities to manipulate the system so they can, again, repeat that stupid act that Darwin hasn't quite taken action on yet.

The stupid that is being referenced in this lesson is a little more complex and involves at least two parties no matter the intelligence, the position, or the intention; it is the actor and the observer. It really takes both.

If, for example, you step in it, no matter what the "it" is, and there are no witnesses and/or you did not realize or cause any lasting effects then, quite logically, it really didn't happen, at least that is how we tend to internalize these occurrences. It has something to do with "if a tree falls in the woods…" and all of that other philosophical mumbo jumbo.

LIFE'S LITTLE LESSONS TOO, A PROPER LIFE WITH A CAREER

Going around telling people about all the stupid things you may have done, just today, is clearly not a favorite pastime, would be boring to most everybody, and possibly put your value as a person into real question. Most likely, there isn't enough time in anyone's day to do both the act along with the play-by-play and still get anything useful done.

What we are down to in this discussion are two specific groups and the people they affect around them. The first are those foolish acts perpetrated by individuals that can best be classified under lack of attention, absentmindedness, or just plain laziness—a kind of induced or indulged ignorance. Darwin can judge these and rule later.

On the other hand, are the people who do things that are clearly stupid and expect to continue to get away with it because they are entitled above reproach or they are higher in the hierarchical pecking order, and so no one take notice. In these cases, some may also think they are simply smarter, at least they think they are, than the individuals around them, and so they pontificate on the subject at hand and expect acceptance of the information through acquiescence.

In all these cases, it is the lack of the observers' willingness to call the foul that continues to perpetuate the problem. In other words, there is a direct inverse correlation between the growth in the number of stupid acts and the ones that are identified as such, particularly when there is a large differential in the social or job-related pecking order.

We easily see this relationship where we work, and sometimes where we play, but we also see them within the ranks of our appointed and elected officials. For whatever the reason, we seem to select, or they self-select, individuals who are completely clueless and clearly not up to the expected or required tasks of their jobs and positions; plus, they can't or won't learn the needed capabilities.

It is bad enough to not have the knowledge or the skill set to do a job. To then expect everyone around you to kowtow to your inadequacies and/or lack of any measurable intelligence is another situation altogether.

Most of the people who fit into this descriptive group pick one of two paths in their operational styles. The first is to appeal to the mercy of their associates or subordinates, learn what is needed and use the combined skill set of the group to most effectively move the effort forward. This would seem to be the preferred path and the one that eventually removes the party from the aforementioned stupid group. Let your past experiences judge the percentage that chooses this option.

The second is to ignore the realities and micromanage the capabilities and skill set of the human and financial resources that are available, given, or assigned to them. Note that they normally will also ask for time extensions and additional resources. Finally, they will find a way to blame everything and everyone around them for their failure to move the effort forward at a reasonable pace, and if they plead their case well enough, they will most likely be rewarded with an advancement with even greater responsibilities that they can't or won't be able to handle in the future. This is often called the "Peter Principle" or some derivation thereof.

This latter situation is clearly too prevalent in our society at all levels of corporate America and, of course, government: local, state, and federal. It is also prevalent in our social programs and the very activities we subject ourselves, and our families too. For a lot of these social activities, people literally get fed up and leave, but the rest are mandated by societal, employment, and governance rules and expectations to put up with the worst of it. Sometimes, we just get jaded or overwhelmed and simply settle for the less than adequate, mediocre results, or less.

Letting "stupid" continue with no relief or recourse is affecting our social climate where we live and work, our creative and innovative talents, and the governance we are expecting and subjecting ourselves to. We shouldn't have a problem with ignorant people who are willing to learn and to do the best they can. The problem is with those who are unwilling to learn or to develop new skill sets but still expect to be allowed by silent assentation to do as they please.

This nonreaction on our part has perpetuated a growing degree of hopelessness and complacency, which has an additional downside. What you get from all this is a breeding of incompetence where equally incompetent people are recruited at all management and leadership levels to insure the "stupid" isn't exposed or jeopardized. More importantly, what you also get is a lowering of the achievement bar that removes the challenge and the need for excellence.

The Lesson

This slowness in the reaction of Mother Nature to cure stupid or reduce our foolishness, of course, is very fortunate for a lot of us since like most this author often frequents the stage for stupid comments and actions. We all do things that later causes us a moment of pause. It is part of who we are and clearly a part of the human condition. For most cases, it is not the act so much as it is our failure to identify and to seek a remedy, and to take heed for the future, that causes us all the cascading problems.

We all do foolish and stupid things, probably more often than we would like to admit, or even want to know. Fortunately, the universe, Mother Nature, luck, or some divine and gracious intelligence simply chooses to let it pass. Not taking that second look at the stoplight or not looking where you are stepping has caught us all, and for some, it has resulted in painful lessons learned: a trip to the hospital, or possibly the morgue, or more often than not, simply nothing at all.

Interestingly, this seems to be how the human process works, and since we seem to somehow survive our actions, or inactions, maybe we shouldn't be quite so critical, or should we?

Most of the stupid or foolish actions that we individually make, no matter the outcome, usually affect only the direct participants or, at most, a predictable few. If you run that red light or knock that cup of hot coffee over onto your colleague's lap, the end result will most likely be confined to a few people, plus the local environment around you.

The reason I get down on myself when I let something of my doing slip through the cracks is not just the concerns that I might have caused bodily injury or property damage, although that would be sufficient, my real concern is that I have yet again not been present of mind for even the simplest things in life. Imagine the impact if those same thoughtless actions affected communities, countries, regions, or for that matter, the globe.

Not that many decades ago, we had a US president speak to us about a kinder and gentler society for America. I don't believe that saying was the start of the current situation since, clearly, stupid has been around since little Jimmy decided to poke the sleeping bear. I do believe, though, that we, as a population, have decided that it is just plain easier to let things continue as they are and to not make trouble correcting it.

This, of course, would be in contrast to stepping up and announcing that something is just plain stupid or being handled by some fool that is overdue for a Darwin strike. Kinder and gentler seems to have become confused with stupid and foolish. We have become a nation of busy people who believe that the way things are was mandated on high, plus, who are we as individuals to question the wisdom, or lack thereof, of the masses.

I don't believe the current masses had any real input into the present situation although they are contributory through their silence. Everywhere I go, and in most everything I read and hear as formal pronouncements, I get this uneasy feeling that what is being pontificated is being listened to by people who are either clueless, uncaring or feel obligated by self-imposed, or job and socially related expectations to sit there and take it. I also believe there are a growing percentage of those participants that do not believe or accept what they see, listen to, or read. The question, then, is why they don't speak up and do what I do and just say, "THIS IS STUPID!"

Unfortunately, I don't have the answer to this question, and in everything I hold sacred, I wish I had at least a glimmer. Maybe what is needed is for just those few who have the presence of mind to just step up and say something. It may possibly require a ground swell to get noticed. All I know is we have a lot of individuals in this world who are still plugged in enough to know when things are not right, or not right enough.

LIFE'S LITTLE LESSONS TOO, A PROPER LIFE WITH A CAREER

Yes, I know we all, especially me, will see and call it wrong every once in a while. I didn't say I don't make mistakes. The reality is that if we haven't made a few mistakes today, we probably haven't done anything good either, or we are still in bed with the covers pulled over our heads. Isn't it time for each of you to identify a small piece of our human foolishness so you can improve the same? Until nature takes notice, I believe we need to become its voice for reason.

The Innovation/ Leadership Impulse

Management may drive the wheels of progress, but leadership chooses the direction, where innovation populates the future landscape.

The Discussion

Historically recognized leadership, and the innovation that resulted from its direct and indirect efforts, was and still is one of the essential components for progress and success. It has often been overlooked developmentally, even more so today than in the past, by the very system that needs it the most.

History books are full of the strong-willed, tenacious, compulsive, focused, charismatic, visionary, and often troubled but, ultimately, successful individuals who, through their very disruptive nature, became the needed leaders and innovators for that time period.

Each was uniquely different stemming from their environmental, social, and economic backgrounds. Most of them faced adversity, financial and physical woes, and often some had serious problems with social and interpersonal relationships. Their common distinguishing set of traits, in addition to those above, included a "fire in the belly" and the inability to resist solving an obvious need or a not-so-clearly defined problem, as well as the ability to lead us, often unwillingly, to a better future.

Looking closer at the history of these individuals, you will find that prior to their documented success, some were frequently regarded less highly and often referred to as scoundrels, dreamers, and more often than not, totally insane, at least from the standpoint of their compulsive attachment to their convictions. They were risk-takers, putting themselves, family, and friends in financial jeopardy, even to the point of sometimes placing their own survival into question.

It is ironic how their ultimate success tended to forgive, forget, or cure all these prior ailments and distractions, along with the previous and often vocal opinions of their detractors. In a lot of these cases, unfortunately, the realization of success was celebrated posthumously. Either way, the history of success has its own selective memory, as it most likely should, since we often don't know what is best for us until viewed through a rearview mirror.

Fortunately for all of us, though, innovation and leadership are not limited to just those few that made the history books or more recently the History Channel. We find evidence of their contributions all around us, and it is normally present in some form in most interactions and transactions that occur continuously in any social environment.

Most of these leadership types will never make the history books, or the evening news for that matter. All of them, though, are essential for more than just our survival. They organize us and provide direction and indirectly, but effectively, provide the needed lubrication that results from the inevitable social friction of just being around each other, not to mention their inane ability to help solve critical resource management issues.

We, as a society, have either been enormously lucky in finding these invaluable individuals in our times of need, and often rescue, or there is a natural order to things that effectively requires that when a problem grows large enough, a needed innovator and leader will rise to meet the challenge.

The general consensus is that there is the potential, often unrealized, in all of us to take the lead and to solve most, if not all, of the problems of the day. It might also be interesting to consider leadership and innovation as an impulse that is triggered by need, perceived or otherwise, a crisis or just possibly an inner urge, like an itch, that needs to be scratched.

It turns out that leadership and innovation surfaces continuously in any number of situations, most likely unpredictably. With the exception of the crisis-based need, most of these awakenings are person and situation-dependent with little or no way to predict their arrivals, at least not using the normal educational and training tools of today.

Similar to a flock of geese flying in formation, the leader is providing the direction and making choices for the group. The leader is also providing additional lifting energy to the two geese next in formation from the shedding vortices on his/her wing tips. As the leader tires in the chosen role, the next goose will move up to take that position allowing the former leader the opportunity to move back into the flock to use their combined parasitic lift to lighten its load, thus providing a respite from the leadership role.

Like in the geese example, leadership is instinctual, and each person can activate that capability if the situation arises, and there is a directed intent from the individual. The reason to step up to that role is not necessarily the result of a crises or a directive. It also comes internally from a need to accomplish something important for the individual and the group they are associated with.

Much like the flock of geese, once a leader picks their path, the rest will join to help push that leader to a destination. Note that the followers are effectively drafting behind the leader, drawing additional strength from the leader's wake.

Innovation can be the leadership driver and for the innovator, it can seem like there is a crisis that must be averted, and they have the solution. For other innovators, the slow and steady approach works even better. The real result for all these individuals is that once on course, they are hard to discourage or deflect. For this and many other reasons, we need them desperately.

The Explanation

This leadership potential, of course, is not to be confused with everyone's desire to be the boss of at least his or her own destinies. The designation of the boss has its own definition, which often involves a change of perceived stature, authority, and of course, the pecking order in the management hierarchy. Leadership seems to fall under the radar in most organizations except within the leader's sphere of influence.

Sometimes those with the strongest leadership skills are kept constrained by a well-managed organization because those leadership characteristics might upset the current structure and/or the reward system within the current management system.

The definition of a boss tends to fit the management side of the equation and while all organizations need bosses to manage the day-to-day work requirements, the essential leader in an organization or any relationship is rarely identified as a boss.

The leader in an organization has been known to forget or ignore the very people they will eventually end up leading. The boss manages the prescribed daily activities while the leader finds a way to solve the bigger problem often altering or eliminating the originally believed best practices.

Additionally, there is most likely a percentage of the population, as history is apt to show us, that have the visionary attributes to not only solve today's problems but also to anticipate the growing issues for tomorrow and to help prepare us for those in a more timely manner than we currently seem to be capable of doing. The "sky is falling" rarely works, and worse, it desensitizes us to the real issues that require long-term and carefully implemented solutions.

Thus, it is the behind-the-scenes proactive leadership that keeps the sky blue and in its proper orientation. They also often tend to keep a cool head when Chicken Little is running around, often because they not only see the actual problem, they also know they can solve that problem should it manifest itself within their sphere of influence.

While most problems come in a variety of sizes and with differing consequences, they all need to be solved and in a timely fashion. Failing to provide timely solutions only exacerbates the problem, and for most situations, it increases the future consequences of the failure.

In most of the cases in the past, the problems and their solutions were generational in nature. In other words, the problem plus the solution had time to incubate; there was time to learn and train the problem solvers, and then there was time to implement the solution—most likely at least one or more generational cycles.

There was also time to allow the populace the comfort interval of acceptance, required to avoid general negative reaction and push back, particularly if the required changes were perceived to be too radical, affecting too many comfort-based lifestyle changes, or it might affect the current vested interest of the status quo.

It should be noted that previous generations handled the cultural, economic, and technological changes better than was expected or anticipated by the then-thought leaders of the day. Consider, for instance, the social and economic changes that occurred due to scientific and engineering spurred technological advancements during the century from 1850 to 1950. Clearly, the landscape of the day changed continuously and dramatically, but no one sailed off the edge of the world.

However, while the local and regional economies were often temporarily disrupted, the improvements, when they were economically successful, were adopted and the region would right itself and flourish again, albeit uniquely different than during their recent past.

In fact, the general population tends to accept and often require the progress caused by change, much faster than is comfortable to the producers of said improvements. It is the essential leaders and innovators who rise out of the ranks that often force the required changes to occur sometimes—often—in spite of the best practices of the day.

The Solution Cycle

Regarding the solution cycle, if society is to accelerate developmentally, the needs for leadership and innovation and the impact that an accelerating and growing population has on social and environmental pressures have shortened the problem-to-solution cycle. The situation has developed to the point that by simply waiting for the next great visionary leader means we are already seriously behind the solution curve. The direct result of this delay will be an increase in both the social and environmental pressures that we will all have to contend with later.

We need to not only find and embrace those few leaders and innovators who will rise to the top naturally; we also need to stimulate, train, and reward any and all who recognize a need and want to brave the normal slings and arrows that result when a person takes the road less travelled, where leadership is one such path, especially those leadership descriptors covered in this lesson.

These leaders in all the categories from the world-class decision-makers to the person that redirects the local civic group, from the backyard mechanic to the office worker or plant and field worker, all help to create the fundamental pathways, plus the guidance to provide social and economic progress and to lessen the pressures when those pathways are not met or are delayed. It is time to pay more attention to their value or at least we should try to stay out of their way, when at all possible.

The current social and educational system, and even within the private and governmental organizations, are at their best and most effective when producing the talents needed for maintaining the current status quo. Finding the visionary leadership and innovators to not only advance, but to also accelerate that advancement should be the fundamental need of any time period. We cannot go back to a simpler time; that ship has sailed. To get to where we are now, required some really tough decisions and some major disruptions to our living conditions and lifestyle.

Technology has provided a means to better social and personal security while also providing the potential for improved longevity and personal satisfaction. Also, it is important to note that as the world's population continues to grow, it will require a growing reliance on advanced technology to maintain and increase the expectations of that better-informed and equipped world population.

The Lesson

Conducting business, and navigating life's pathways for that matter, is ever-changing and ever-advancing. Enhanced visionary leadership is critical if we are to progress and stay ahead of the problems, we create by simply taking up space on this planet. Meeting these growing needs and expectations will only happen if we recognize that change is a fundamental requirement for any progressive system, and in general, that change will not be obvious to those individuals immersed in the current problem-set of the day.

The individuals who are best at identifying and mentoring these essential individuals are they themselves leaders and innovators. Enhanced leadership, plus the innovators, as a developed skill set needs to be identified and placed where it can do the most good, solving the problems we continuously create. The following was prepared to put these thoughts into a succinct form:

Leadership

> Leadership without innovation promotes the short term while neglecting the future. Innovation without leadership is undirected, needlessly expending resources while eroding stakeholder value. With both, you get vision, planning, and confidence to overcome the hurdles brought on by progress and change.

Managing Committees

There is a reason and need for strong leadership.
The best a committee does is to acquire information,
And the worse, to hide and mitigate potential liabilities.

The Discussion

It turns out most formal organizations and even loosely organized groups, to be successful, end up with some form of a management core and a formalized structure. Sometimes the structure forms up as a result of a perceived need or as a visionary response from one of the initial participants. Other times, the mission is part of a larger group of activities and while the object may be clear, the task orders, timeline, and use of resources may need focus and direction. This appears to be the natural order to human activities, and often, we see similar activities in the animal kingdom where there is a boss or leader to help align resources and, for most cases, to increase survivability.

Even when there isn't a recognized position of authority, inevitably someone assumes the mantle of boss, leader, or manager even if only to function in that position for a brief period. It is human nature for everyone to see the obvious in a slightly different way, and as a result, if someone doesn't assume the role of taking the responsibility to organize and direct the group's resources, then the initial purpose and goal for the group may go astray. This, of course, assumes that a proper amount of authority is also provided for the management of those resources. Thus, with a perceived authority, or one granted by member accommodation, the organization can proceed with a goal-based plan.

It turns out most groups of individuals recognize the need to form up behind leadership whether it is a formal position or a temporary one that resulted from an immediate need or crisis. Similar to a flock of geese flying in formation, the leader is providing the direction and making decisions for the group. The leader is also providing lifting energy to the geese next in formation from the shedding vortices on its wing tips. As it tires, in the leadership role, the next goose will move up to take that role allowing the former leader the opportunity to move back into the flock to use their parasitic lift to lighten its load.

Like for the geese example form earlier lessons, leadership is effectively instinctual, and each person can activate that capability if the situation arises, and there is a needed intent from the individual or the group, they have assimilated. The reason to step up to that role is not necessarily the result of a crises or a directive. It may also come internally from a need to accomplish something important and useful for the individual and the group they are a part of.

Everyone seemingly knows what a boss is, and it could be that we recognize them without introductions simply by their presence, attitude, and stature. The same applies to leadership, but the difference is often in the end result where the leader may have the vision for a new goal, but the boss most likely will be charged in organizing the resources to get to the originally intended goal, on time and under budget. Noting that this lesson is not on the specific differences or commonalities between bosses and leaders; suffice it to say they both define a form of authority and responsibility to complete an envisioned set of tasks.

There are some very good-to-great bosses and some, well, not so much. The latter group are normally referred to as equivalent to diapers—always on your back and often full of crap. The better end of the spectrum is normally appreciated and often well respected and regarded as essential to job completion by both the upper management and the direct reports who work under them. A similar spectrum can be defined for leaders with some very good ones to the not so good, which history has reported on in detail for all of these types of individuals.

The Explanation

The purpose of this lesson actually has very little to do with bosses or any kind of leadership and more on the purposes of committees, although sometimes, they all get intertwined. The discussions on leadership are covered somewhat in lesson 22, although it would take a full-blown textbook to adequately cover the definitions and generalizations of these two distinct groups. Committees, on the other hand, are a little simpler to define and understand. From the *Merriam-Webster's* definition: "a committee is a body of persons delegated to consider, investigate, take action on, or report on some matter."

From this definition, it is clear that most committees are formed up to gather information and intelligence on a topic to help, and possibly enhance, a decision-maker's ability to provide more effective management of the resources and ultimately the direction of an organization. As with bosses and leaders, the management core, there are good committees and, again, the not so good. Sometimes, the lack of effectiveness of a committee is simply a bad mix of the personalities or the knowledge base of the participants who make up the group. At other times, it is the directions provided by the management seeking their assistance or possibly the designated leadership within the committee itself.

In recent years, some committees have been formed representing diverse constituencies within an organization to help encourage, and sometimes force, a consensus within the entire organization. Thus, the committee is being used to perform the decision-maker's job where the blame or backlash from the decision is on the shoulders of the committee members and not the management.

While this use of a committee may lighten the responsibilities of the manager, it asks the committee and its individual members to carry the grievance pushback from the rank and file, which is most likely not in their job description, plus they are being asked to assume the responsibility for the decision without the authority to modify or correct any of the resulting consequences, the concepts here were partially covered in lesson 4.

Sometimes, committees are formed to stall the making of a decision. In this situation, the management is most likely directing or interfering with the actions of the committee and if that manager doesn't like the direction the committee outcome might take, then they will simply alter the charge to the committee to redirect and delay the outcome. Management, by its definition, is responsible to direct the personnel and physical resources of an organization. Not all decisions are the best, and few are the worse but using the organizational resources to delay or redirect the goals of the organization when the decisions might not be popular is not effective. It is particularly grievous when a committee is being misused because the decision that is being discussed is not in the best interest of the manager or might be in conflict with the special outside interests of the powers-to-be.

The other equally irresponsible use of a committee, particularly if the self-appointed committee leadership is also the manger that created the committee in the first place, is its use to mitigate the fallout from the decisions being implemented by the committee. The notion of a manager mitigating the impact of what should have been the manager's decision through the use of a committee is reprehensible. Some committees are deliberating formed to mitigate the fallout from the decisions that were already in place or soon to be placed, thus forcing the committee members to assume the final consequences of any of the decisions that were already known or decided upon by the manager.

In all cases, when individuals are taken away from their assigned job tasks to form up a committee charged to expedite a decision-making process, the outcome is typically a positive use of their time plus it allows some controlled and informative interactions among diverse membership within an organization. Unfortunately, when the use of a committee is to delay or derail a process or to force a consensus among disparate groups, the outcome at best is a misuse of resources and, at worse, a dereliction of duties.

What most managers often don't understand is that when committee members are used in this negative fashion, the stress of the entire organization increases. Additionally, while the manager in question may appear immune from any backlash, especially from their superiors, the direct reports will ultimately figure the situation out and either vote with their feet or act out their stress in nonproductive, work-related ways.

The Lesson

Committees by their nature and definition are effective vehicles to get decisions made in expedient ways. Their misuse, because a decision-maker isn't capable of managing properly or because a specific decision might not be in the manager's best interest, is a travesty and a total misuse of the committee's resources.

Always look to the committee charge when asked to join a committee. If it appears management is looking for the information needed to make a responsible decision, then most likely, it is a good use of your time. If not, then you should try to find a way out of this situation, or at least you should try to mitigate the negative impact the manager in question is trying to create at your expense and the overall expense of the organization.

I should caution everyone who gets involved in one of these less-than-admirable committee situations that any manager who is willing to improperly use organizational resources to avoid, derail, or alter the intent of an upcoming decision, is also capable of vindictive actions against anyone perceived to not be cooperating with their designs. In other words, tread lightly but also be responsible to the organization you are representing, even if the current manager isn't.

30. Economic Indicators

The progress train has left the station.
It is too late to go back now.

The Discussion

The following lesson is a culmination of many of the engineering aspects I learned and then taught to scores of my students. It is included with these lessons mainly to satisfy my need to pontificate on what I think I understand about the technological base in this country. While most of my lessons in life occurred at a specific time, or at least over a brief period, the contents in this lesson have been coming on since I was a kid, growing up with a father who worked in the energy industry, and then subsequently accelerating as I started and continued my career in engineering, where mobility and the energy to move it were the subjects of my studies.

I will have to say that I have been blessed with the opportunity to work on numerous energy and mobility-related projects over the length of my career and, more importantly, to have had the opportunity to learn from some of the best energy experts in the world on these topics. I have had opportunities to work on a variety of wind turbines, solar collector arrays, and even solar cells. I have worked in most of the carbon-based energy systems and even published a paper on nuclear energy. I have also worked or studied most of the mobility systems that are in current use or are proposed for the near future. So please bear with me while I try to transfer a smattering of some of my learnings to each of you, my readers.

In all these studies, the key elements were, and still are, energy and mobility. It is what heats, cools, cooks, protects, and moves us; plus, it does the same for all of the essential elements that allow us to live the way we do. How we acquire, transport, and use that energy plus how we clean up the results of that use will determine how successful we will be as a species going into the future.

The need for increasing amounts of energy will continue as the population grows and also as a result of energy equalization among the various countries and regions on this planet. The differential between the "haves" and the "have-nots" will continue to shrink as acquired knowledge and communication capabilities increase. In all these discussions, the indicators that stand out are mobility, the transportation sector, and energy, the theme of this lesson.

Mobility in any of its forms is often regarded as the standard and trademark for social and economic progress. The movement of people, goods, and even information is at the heart of our social and economic systems, particularly in the United States, but generally worldwide.

It is in the transportation sector, in addition to moving life's essentials, where we will see our greatest economic growth. A solid and reliable transportation system backed by sufficient and reliable energy supplies also act to stabilize an economy and thus transportation, and the infrastructure to support it, is often at the heart of any modern and evolving society.

While the transportation process may have started from one individual moving goods and information to another, the process quickened through the domestication of beasts of burden and then on to more transformational forms of transportation. These included wagons and then rail cars and ships and so on to include over-the-road vehicles in a variety of sizes and purposes.

Air travel heralded in a new era of fast and cost-effective transportation for people and goods. The telephone and other communication systems, including satellites sped up the transfer of information and thus helped to minimize the overall transportation costs.

In all of these technologies, even employing the use of animals, the effort has always been to make the process more energy-efficient while minimizing costs. The key here may not be the actual final direct costs but the total energy requirements to support the developing economy.

The Role of Innovation

Innovation has always been the driving force behind humanity's success at conquering our environment and in advancing our social agendas, as I have written about multiple times in this book. In that ongoing effort, it is the acquisition and utilization of energy and the transportation using that energy that has allowed us to advance and create better and more fulfilling lifestyles.

This lesson looks at the genesis of innovation in the United States and how the US's progression to a global powerhouse occurred due to both the human and environmental resources created as a result of the survival instincts associated with innovation. If this nation, and those that are mirroring it, are going to continue to make economic and social improvements and advancements, then the leaders and innovators of the world are going to play a critical part in that effort, and energy will power and move those improvements.

The United States has always held a prominent place globally in fostering innovation, as is exemplified in the worldwide consumer acceptance of its technology and products. This innovation has also cultivated, attracted, and provided the incentives for a strong leadership core that has served the nation in the best and worst of economic times. Similarly, to many regions of this country, it was with the cultural diversity and open-market spirit, facilitated by the availability of natural resources, that the US's innovative vision was forged, providing the driving force for social, cultural, and economic change.

To this day, it is the interplay of these attributes and resources that creates our dynamic cultural and social heritage and provides a standard of living that has few global equals. The nation initially benefited from its many unique geographic and resource-rich regions.

It also benefited from the changing cultural and demographic attributes influenced by the growing and diverse population.

The risk-takers, adventurers, and individuals looking for a better, more prosperous life all contributed to the changing landscape that became the US. Each brought their language and culture and, more importantly, a variety of trade skills and a willingness to learn, adapt, and work hard because there was a clear avenue to a fair financial exchange for their contributions, plus a sense of accomplishment for their efforts.

The skill set requirements for each local industry and trade, along with the local energy-rich environments, influenced the specific influx of families and their languages and cultures. This, in turn, provided natural population and cultural centers matched to the local intellectual and capital-rich environments. Many of these individuals were attracted by the opportunities created by these cultural and political dynamics while others had the needed skills or a vision of what the future could provide, and they wanted to be a part of that change.

These highly productive regions, located throughout the country, started as natural offshoots from the geographic attributes and natural resources that were available. From the grass lands, that even now feed this nation as well as many other nations around the world, to the safe harbors that ring the coastline, including the Great Lakes, it was from these starting points that the nation got its initial foundations. These regions grew and prospered and with that growth came the need for better and faster transportation and the energy to drive it.

This need for transportation was not just necessary for the required exchanges in commerce but also for the people who were attracted to the ever-growing and changing opportunities that this new landscape was providing. Even at the beginning, it was the movement of people, products, and information, along with the concomitant development of new sources of energy, that kept the wheels of industry and commerce moving, as it still does today. Each region can claim, and often boast of, its place in the historical development of this country.

Today, these regions continue to contribute, responding through changes in their work and living environments and often adjusting their roles in the constantly evolving global marketplace. Now, energy plus the movement of people, products, and information is occurring on a larger, more profound scale and to compete in the worldwide marketplace requires a broader view and a global perspective.

These new types of global dynamics, similar to the regional ones in the past, are fraught with complexities, discomfort, and personal insecurity, but as in the past, there is an inevitableness to these changes that will require the population to adapt and learn to take on this next round of opportunities.

Embracing Change

It is in the embrace of change where innovative breakthroughs occur, and it was those earlier breakthroughs that propelled this country into the world leadership position it has held for so many decades. While change can often feel undesirable, it is the natural, inevitable, and necessary order of the universe. Maintaining the status quo may seem to make life easier, but in reality, it allows competing forces to gain a foothold or to get ahead.

When you are in the lead, everyone wants to contribute their intellectual energy and products to your vision; they want to come and make themselves part of the mix. When you lose your edge or get behind, that same innovation, and the leadership that spawned it, goes elsewhere.

When it comes to change, most everyone speaks to it as a necessity, as long as it doesn't adversely affect them personally or what they are doing. Change comes in two major varieties: the revolutionary breakthroughs and the subtler evolutionary transformations that slowly infiltrate the workplace and living environment.

The latter is all around us, with visible examples in the communications and medical industries. The same can be said for all sectors of the work environment, where these advancements are more dramatic for some sectors than for others. This transformation is a slowly evolving process that the nation has grown accustomed to, often to the point of not even seeing the change—or worse, often missing the vision that is driving that innovation—until it is well established.

This missed vision, particularly for breakthrough innovations, is not without its negatives, as exemplified with the loss of jobs, personal initiative, and in general, a loss in the innovative spirit due to not seeing or anticipating future trends and needs, particularly on a global basis. Having at least a limited vision of the future is a prerequisite if this country is to compete in a global marketplace.

Fortunately, as a society, we entrust those few which have been identified as innovators with the power to shape a larger, more radical view of the future that lies ahead. The innovative breakthroughs, or gamechangers, are the easiest to detect, as they usually affect large segments of the population and work environments. Each of these changes will require a greater commitment of energy and the mobility infrastructure to develop it. Plus, that energy and the resulting technology will have to move to meet the needs of the population.

As is normally the case, these changes are often opposed by individuals and companies alike simply because they represent something different, such as a change from the current direction of their organization that forces them out of their comfort zone. Resistance, in and of itself, isn't necessarily bad because inertia provides the time to adjust and, more importantly, to become proactive as opposed to always being reactive.

Whatever the process, change is inevitable, and this nation's population has the choice of embracing that change, as our forefathers did and who also looked forward to it, or unfortunately letting the rest of the world adapt and accelerate those same changes to best fit their current needs and desires, often to our disadvantage. It is through energy and mobility that allows for our continued success. We just need to take charge of both of these to keep us viable.

LIFE'S LITTLE LESSONS TOO, A PROPER LIFE WITH A CAREER

The Lesson

There are two considerations that increase the domestic fuel-use opportunity by several orders of magnitude—the offset in the use of nondomestic fuels with the associated retained revenues plus the innovation that comes during any technological and cultural change.

The first of these is obvious. We have in the past sent almost a trillion dollars a year out of country for our liquid fuel supplies, including the cost associated with our military and diplomatic corps to keep those supplies secure. The impact has been a continual drag on our economy and our workforce, an unmanageable trade deficit, and an inability of our nation to stay out of the political interests of the rest of the globe.

These dollars retained at home could pay for life's essentials and the joys that have been the hallmark of our existence. By keeping this money at home, we increase our tax base and our ability to purchase and spend resources for our own benefit. It furthers our ability to increase our social and financial infrastructure. Infusing millions, if not billions of dollars, back into our local economies would provide the healing we clearly need as a nation.

The second of these two may prove to be just as dramatic. We, as a nation, have always pushed the envelope when we saw the need. It is an essential part of our heritage and most likely part of our social genetic makeup. The definition of innovation is change. While change is often uncomfortable, it nevertheless is an essential requirement if we are to progress as a society.

We have managed to stay somewhat dormant for the past several decades, and while it may have seemed the comfortable solution, the rest of the world has not simply sat by and watched; they have raced to advance their technological and cultural base, often with a leapfrog over the normal steps in a progressing technology, thus saving them resources and critical time. They have learned well from our efforts, which means we have to work even harder to get and stay ahead.

To get ahead will mean a change in our social infrastructure or a movement back to the maverick, shoot from the hip, innovative genius that we used to look for and reward, and still have buried in the hearts of our next generation of leaders and innovators. We need to bring our capital home and put it to work, creating the competitive edge our people are most capable of producing.

We also need to help by providing the appropriate venues for the innovators to come to the surface and then to help them get their ideas into the marketplace. In a large number of cases, the focus will be in the energy and mobilities sectors. Who would have thought that the movement of people and goods could change the economic landscape of a nation—it always has.

Future Mobility Drivers

We are all effectively energy in one form or another.

Personal Experience

Most of my professional career has involved topics related to mobility. While most of my earlier lessons in this book have related to personal and social development, my later experiences have been more of a technical nature. It should be noted that these technical lessons have also impacted my personal life, not just my career. Acquiring the technical information plus the skills related to the disciplines I have dealt with, have also crafted who I have become. Information in general tends to do that to a person and so I have provided some of that information here for you to absorb and ponder.

The Discussion

A growing percentage of mobility experts contend that transportation in the future will rely primarily on electric drives, in contrast to the mechanical drives we predominately use today. It is still unclear as to the final form these drives will take and how each mobility sector will incorporate their use, but in the future, mobility power will most likely be measured in kilowatts and not just horsepower.

All of this is predicated, though, on a series of innovative breakthroughs in a variety of disciplines including intelligent vehicles and highways, increased on-board energy storage capacity, and of course, an evolutionary change in the consumer mindset, to name only a few.

Most locomotives and even some ships have gone to electric drives along with a growing number of commuter-sized vehicles that rely in some part on the direct conversion of electrical energy into mechanically driven work; current examples include hybrids and electric vehicles.

Most of these innovations for small vehicles have been on the drawing boards and on the test tracks for years. They have been waiting for the consumer and commercial markets to catch up with the improvement potentials of these applications. The original equipment manufacturers (OEMs) are also waiting for that next technology breakthrough to help make these products more commercially viable, thus profitable. All of this is, of course, linked to the requirements and sometime demands of the customer who can be influenced to look at new technology as long as it isn't too costly or wasteful, and it isn't too hard to operate and maintain.

The current lack in the widespread implementation of these advanced technologies is effectively the same as it has been for the past one hundred years; it is really hard to beat the energy content and at-the-pump cost of petroleum-based products, especially considering the current well-developed storage and distribution infrastructure that is already in place in this country. In fact, if worldwide fuel availability, and the environmental consequences of its use, were not an issue and the cost could be kept low, then petroleum would be a hard fuel source to beat, measured against almost any standard. This assumes that we would continue to address and meet the emissions requirements from its use plus the worldwide environmental impact caused by the recovery, delivery, and distribution of these nonrenewable energy resources.

The OEMs have and will continue to meet the ever-increasing emissions requirements, and they will also continue to improve the efficiency of the current vehicles by reducing weight, improving aerodynamics, increasing combustion efficiency and adding a myriad of intelligent controls that will continue to advance and improve the safety of transportation, the lifeline of a modern society.

What is most interesting is that each advancement in the state of the art for conventional mobility—cars, trucks, boats, and trains—also enhances even more advanced vehicles; the ones that the experts are predicting for the not-so-distant future. In fact, it appears that even with an adequate supply of economically priced petroleum, these improvements will move mobility unceasingly toward vehicles that require ever greater amounts of electrical power, which will be increasingly used in the direct propulsion of the vehicle. The question in the future then becomes, where will that power originate?

The nature of a mobility enterprise in a free society has always been directed to the creation and fielding of a variety of new, advanced vehicles, which in recent times have progressively started using more nontraditional technologies, such as wheel motors, hybrids, and even flex-fuels plus all-electrics, etc. The domestic and now global competition to build the next better vehicle will continue to favor the more efficient and greener vehicle, and thus, to stay commercially competitive, these companies will try to anticipate future needs, to mitigate liabilities and to gain a competitive edge, all while satisfying and appealing to the changing needs, and sometimes unpredictable wants, of the consumer.

Energy and Mobility

Unfortunately, the availability and acquisition of inexpensive liquid fuels, that we have based our economy on for so many decades, are becoming more than a little problematic. While we can't ignore the direct impact that sending over a billion dollars a day out-of-country, for the purchase of those fuel reserves, has had on our economy and the value of our dollar, it has also resulted in the loss of jobs, infrastructure neglect and decay, and a decline in the driving force behind innovation in this country, especially among our young people.

Some would say that even these issues pale in comparison to the loss of life and the diverted resources that are used to protect our political interests and the acquisition of nondomestic energy supplies in volatile areas around the world. Putting our soldiers in harm's way to protect our rights, interests, and needs to be mobile would only be justified if there was no recourse, which isn't the case anymore since we have the needed energy reserves within our borders.

In fact, those in the know would say we have always had those reserves, but for whatever the reasons—financial; convenience; or reacting to legal, political, and legislative realities—we have historically chosen to go offshore for the majority of our energy needs. Even those who contend that we didn't have the technology to explore, discover, and extract that energy remain silent when it is pointed out that the current and lauded over, as recent technology advances—horizontal drilling and hydro-fracturing—have been around and available for decades.

The nondomestic petroleum that we have based our economy on for the last several generations is not unlimited, and in fact, the analysts are saying that the recoverable quantity has peaked and will slowly decline over the next decade or so. Add to this, the needs of a growing industrial base in the Far East makes what's left ripe for a price war with other countries.

Note that these other developing countries have not yet bled themselves dry economically sending their energy money out of country and who do not mind paying a higher energy price, for a while, since they have an energy plan in place and will only need this nondomestic fuel until their own energy reserves are fully developed. Energy is everywhere around and under us. With money and know-how, that energy can be extracted and utilized. The developing nations around the globe are using the same technology to advance their economies as we have created and are starting to use for ourselves.

So where does this leave us? Some would say we are destined to continue our current downward spiral-like course economically. Continuing to send our capital out of country will result in higher product and food costs and a further diversion of our manufacturing base and jobs out of country. Even worse would be the continuing lack of motivation within our youth who contain the innovative spirit and limitless energy to move this country forward. For it is in them that innovation will spring forth, once they see the need and the unencumbered rewards that can be achieved in a free-market economy. Others would say this is not the reality, that we are going to take back our preeminent position in the world and do it as a motivated population.

Free Enterprise and Mobility

Fortunately, free enterprise in this country has not been sitting on its laurels. These industries, through their leadership, have been predicting the inevitable stress on our economic system that has resulted, at least in part, from relying on nondomestic energy supplies. They have diversified their development efforts, looking at a variety of energy acquisition and improved mobility solutions, each seeking to be more energy efficient.

These forward-looking enterprises will now ramp up the development of these ongoing design concepts as contrasted to trying to start from scratch a developmental program that would normally take years and often decades to mature. It is encouraging to note that a free market continues to thrive even when it is under financial stress, probably one of the better reasons too.

The better leadership in this country believes that we are on track to retake our position in the World because of the very issues that have been mentioned here. The reasons OEMs and their supporting manufacturers have been advancing mobility technology, in spite of the current low cost of fuel and in direct opposition to the apparent desires of the consumer, is because they knew the day would come that fuel availability and cost and the need for better, safer, and more environmentally appropriate vehicles would become publicly preferred and mandated.

They also understood that up until now the state of the art wasn't matured enough to supply the myriad of required vehicles exclusively using electricity. The current power grid cannot support any appreciable increases in consumption that would result from going to all-electric vehicles, even if those vehicles were economically feasible using currently available technology. Additionally, the battery technology, while maturing, is far from offsetting the energy storage capacity in petroleum-based products. Similar discussions can be held on technologies like fuel cells and biofuels where each will make small contributions in their own way to our energy production and use plans in the future.

The apparent answer to near-future mobility appears to rest with the very people and organizations that propelled us into the twentieth and now the twenty-first century, the commercial and industrial centers and their leadership. Advancing technology and making a paradigm shift in the way we do business, in this case, how we move products and people, is a complicated process that should be influenced and directed by need and affordability, and not through artificially contrived or ill-informed mandates.

It is clear that we are not yet prepared to roll out on a large scale a pure electric vehicle fleet that has the range and features as currently offered by a petroleum-based vehicle. Please note that when comparing needs of a transportation system, the average use and distance traveled are key considerations. This country with its large land masses requires vehicles with ranges not required in many other parts of the world. Suffice it to say, each region has differing requirements and needs most of which can be handled with small changes to the mobility platform in question. The problems we need to balance are not necessarily just with the vehicle, they rest more with the developing infrastructure required to support these overall system changes.

That is not to say it can't or won't get done; it will just require an appropriate amount of development time, and almost surely, it will be affected by consumer desires and legislative mandates. In fact, the current process of developing and producing hybrids in all of their current forms are the strategic next steps that will allow us to meet the needs of the consumer, and our society, while staying conscious of the demands for greater fuel economy and an improved environmental impact.

LIFE'S LITTLE LESSONS TOO, A PROPER LIFE WITH A CAREER

The Economics of Change

Since economics plays an important role in introducing new technology, it would be an appropriate exercise to consider the impact that mandating the introduction of an all-electric fleet would have on the price of these vehicles, plus the overall cost to the consumer. Increasing production would require the increased use of rare earths, the majority of which are sourced non-domestically, again putting us in a position of sending our money out of country. The same discussion would center around all of the onboard electronics and a considerable amount of the fabrication materials.

An all-electric fleet would require a major change in our vehicle service capabilities. Not to mention a retiring of a significant portion of our current vehicle service expertise. This is, of course, similar to retiring the horse and buggy industry but with a difference in need for expediency and the training of a new workforce. Depending on the customer-based or governmental mandates this electric vehicle integration could happen in a period of a few years in contrast with earlier revolutionary changes that had a generation to accommodate.

These considerations are only based on the actual vehicle. Currently, the electric grid in this country could not support the rapid introduction of an all-electric fleet. While given sufficient time it could gear up for the increased vehicle needs, but the cost per kilowatt would be substantially increased to meet these needs. Note also that the local utility companies would have to increase capacity in almost every neighbor since their service lines and the supporting equipment was designed for current customer use. This would also require the long-term development of additional generating capacities and the associated needs and costs of raw materials.

Since we are hypothesizing, and we are always looking for that next great battery solution, consider the impact an efficiency breakthrough would have on our petroleum-based transportation choices. Consider what doubling, or possibly tripling, the current over-the-road mileage of our mobility fleet would have on our mobility choices. Cutting fuel use would help keep our money in country and allow our current domestic energy production to meet our energy needs. This breakthrough would also help with the environmental issues of using these fuel sources.

Appling the same hypothetical to a battery that would have an increased storage capacity of at least two to three times that which is currently available today, which is still short of the energy capacity of petroleum, would be a game-changer and clearly move us to using all-electric drives. It would also hasten the implementation of these vehicles, and of course, we would then have no choice but to improve our electrical generating infrastructure. Unfortunately, that improved battery is not yet available while the ability to improve the efficient use of petroleum-based products is still under constant development.

There has always been an economic advantage in using the current petroleum-based fuels to power our economy; remember, it is hard to beat the energy content of a gallon of gasoline. Environmental concerns have required us to make major changes in how we use our energy supplies. The results of this have seen an improvement in overall fuel efficiency and a resultant decrease in measurable pollutants. The question now becomes what happens if petroleum use is cut in half and electric vehicles cost us, as the consumer, considerably more to operate than the same petroleum-based products.

The way innovation happens there is no way to predict where the next great breakthrough will occur, or when, but undoubtably, it will. As the old saying goes, necessity is the mother of invention. As part of that necessity there needs to be a cradle-to-grave analysis for any new technology. We have a terrible habit of reacting to some ill-conceived or an emotionally driven crises without considering the long-term consequences of those decisions.

Actually, several of the implemented, environmentally friendly, energy choices have been shown to have long-term environmental consequences that we, or our children, will have to contend with in the future. In fact, there appears to be a direct correlation between the efficient and effective capabilities of these technologies and the level of the government-funded subsidies required to make them attractive enough to implement.

The consumer ends up paying for these decisions twice, once through higher taxes and then in the higher costs required to implement these technologies by the local providers. Again, most of these problems can be mitigated with a required cradle-to-grave evaluation. More importantly, these types of analyses will help to put facts in front of the decision makers and not just the emotional appeals.

Domestic Energy Sources

Going back to the original discussion, the dwindling nondomestic petroleum fuel sources will also allow us to take increased advantage of the domestic energy supplies that we have to date only started to exploit. These reserves, specifically shale oil and gas, will help to offset the demands for nondomestic supplies leaving more cash on the table in-country and allowing us as a nation to regain control over our economic destiny through self-sufficiency and the innovation encouragement we will pass on to our youth.

Interestingly, the addition of this shale fuel reserves helps to lessen the financial strangle hold that we have suffered under for decades while still fitting into a mobility strategy that can now use natural gas as the fuel of choice for over-the-road fleets and for the direct electricity production in power plants. All of this, of course, should be in preparation for a well-planned and timely transition to all electric vehicles, which is starting to occur even today.

The Lesson

The sun in our solar system provides all the energy we use on this planet in one form or another. It nourishes the crops we grow, the development of the flora and fauna around us, it provides the constantly changing weather patterns, and over the eons, it has provided the sunlight for the materials used in the production of the petroleum products we currently utilize. We are all effectively energy in one form or another, and we use energy external from our bodies to pursue those activities related to our survival and continued social development.

The future success of this species will be directly coupled to how we access and utilize the energy around us. Independent of how we move people, materials, and information, energy will be the driver and if there is a lesson here it is in understanding your relationship to this energy system and process and how you can impact its availability and use.

We are physically here because of the one source that provides all of the energy we have used and will use into the foreseeable future, the sun. If you want to be productive in your short stay on this planet, you will need to understand your personal role in, and potential contributions to, this process.

Never Quit When You Are Down

Make your commitments through your decision-making. Know when to change those decisions and don't hesitate.

The Discussion

As you read this book, I am sure that some, if not most, of what you have read has resonated with you, at least to some extent. Life kind of provides all of us with numerous opportunities to teach us the fundamentals of surviving within our environment, as well as with each other. Often, it's the surviving with the others around us that is the most troublesome and, at times, risky.

These lessons were some I had to live through and learn from, clearly some I learned better than others. While these were but a few of the many I survived, they were nonetheless important then as they are even today. Learning these lessons allowed a deepening of my appreciation of the life I have lived, and the one I hope to continue to live, along with the role I needed to assume to make a contribution to this personal journey.

As with all living creatures, there are moments that stress us to the limit, sometimes putting our very survival in question. Even the less stressful events when added cumulatively can place our survival in question often placing our health in jeopardy or distracting our attention away from a better direction or a safer decision. All this means if we are not attentive enough, we may miss opportunities or get run over by a truck because we didn't look both ways.

This is kind of the reality of our existence, and while our lives are often tenuous at best, we do manage to survive and learn from our mistakes. In fact, the lessons we learn from, especially the ones that move us forward, are often decisions that we make sometimes without a true goal or intent behind the decision.

Admittedly, our brains are always engaged even when we are unaware of our actions and decisions consciously. This is often the case when I wake up with an answer or an idea that I had trouble coming with before I went to sleep. Seems there is some computing power still on when I am blissfully asleep and dreaming about my next great adventure. I suspect we often have input from some portion of our cognitive resources that puts a bug in our ear, or a distress in our bellies, about what we should be doing, or, in some cases, not doing.

The question I have always had, and one that should be posed to everyone is, how much of our survival mode thinking occurs in opposition to what we may consciously think is the correct answer or direction, and how much is in agreement. Or possibly worse is the quiet parts of our brain a better defender from everyday crisis than we are even when we think we are focused and attentive. I suspect the answer is most likely, maybe both. This, of course, may be one of the protective designs in our mental system, and since we have been so successful at survival over the eons, maybe it is best that we just accept that we are what we are and get on with it.

The other alternative is that the brain with all of its capacities is still open to influences both form the cognitive process within as well as those cues that come from other humans and even our environment. Somehow, though, we tend to make a slew of decisions every day and are still around to have that next dream about future exploits. In all these life processes, we gain from these experiences whether good or not-so-good, and if we pay attention the better decisions become more prevalent.

This is sometimes called the learning experience, and too often, it is described as hard-knock wisdom. I suspect everyone has some of these stories to tell, if they ended up positive or possibly not told if not-so-positive. Either way, we learn and hopefully we do better with each processed decision-making event. The following is a little story that helped me put a description to those decision-making events. I have included it here so that every time you hear these words you will remember to think with all of your being as to the best decision-making path to take.

The Story

One of the lessons in this book, lesson 12, spoke to the three types of decisions, which is a saying and a concept I have taken to heart during my career. If I have erred in that thought it was most likely in not taking sufficient time to weigh the presented options. If you remember that was also part of the "haste makes waste" doctrine. Assuming I wasn't too hasty, then the decisions made were the best I could have made at the time, given the information that was then available to me.

During this learning process, and my evolving maturation process, a process that is far from over according to my wife and children, I have always hoped that the decisions made were the best for me and the other individuals that were impacted around me. Clearly, not all these decisions could have been correct, but with most, there was sufficient time allowed for appropriate corrections to improve the opportunity or to at least minimize the downside.

Lest we get confused, the passing of time has a way of showing us the better decisions from the not-so-good ones. I am trying not to use a reference to the term bad decisions since I believe the really bad ones are the ones not made. So if you will indulge me a little, these are the not-so-good ones. I always hoped that staying on top of these decisions going forward would allow for the time needed to correct the not-so-good decisions or to at least reduce the damage, thus the three types of decisions.

The process of making decisions is complex and wrought with difficulties. Some of the problems result from a vested interest in the outcome for yourself or for those around you. It could also result from a misunderstanding of the potential outcomes from that decision. The negative impact that will have to be dealt with downstream of the final decision is yet another.

These are just a few of the complexities that can result during and after a decision is made. In all of these situations, though, once there is a clear route to the best decision, then the choice has to be made and made expediently for everyone's benefit. It is almost like removing a Band-Aid. Pull that sucker off of the skin as quickly as is safely possibly. In the long run, it is less painful; plus, it reduces the trepidation.

There is another part of this decision-making process that reflects directly on this discussion but has other implied outcomes. These are the decisions made that end up with a consequence that must be dealt with. It is easy to get vested in an idea or a process that you have become fundamentally attached to. No matter how many decisions you make during the day, particularly those that have an ongoing process attached to it, some of those decisions will not be the best ones for you to stay invested in. Clearly, the longer we are with a situation, the more invested we can become, for whatever the reasons. It is these long-term or personal issues and situations that can be the hardest to rectify or correct and even harder to get rid of.

This issue is not to be confused with the situation of having unexpected problems or because your involvement has to increase exponentially to handle the developing problems that you contributed to by agreeing on the decision to go forward. There is very little opportunity to look into the future to see the actual requirements for a project, process, or a decision to go forward. It is also evident that the more complex the process, the more there will be unexpected delays, added requirements, and pushback. In fact, I have yet to see the results of a serious decision for a major project go completely as scheduled.

Most of these difficulties are standard, everyday run-of-the-mill reality. Just because things got tough and your expected involvement has to grow to meet the challenges, created by your involvement, doesn't mean the decision was bad and often it is the difficulties and how everyone reacts to them that prove the value of the original idea. So remember, if "the going gets tough, the tough get going," which is a saying attributed to both President John F. Kennedy's father and American coach K. Rockne. I have yet to see an important project get instituted that didn't also have a plethora of associated problems that had to be dealt with if the effort was to become successful.

Clearly, though, this needs to be contrasted with the decisions that were the not-so-good ones with the growing number of difficulties that are only getting worse as the project continues. These are the situations that, like the three decisions lesson, needs to be dealt with as quickly as possible before irrevocable damage is done, or resources are expended that could have been used more wisely for other projects and ideas. These are often difficult decisions to make, but they are even more important than the original ones that put you in this position in the first place.

For these situations, you most likely have known for a while the need to make a change in your decision long before you put it into words. Also, that portion of your nonsleeping brain has most likely been chewing over the situation longer than you started thinking formally about it. It has most likely also been yelling in your ear and causing stressful nights of sleep. Once you know what you have to do, then we are back to the Band-Aid situation and the need to make a prompt decision. I will note to the reader my difficulty in making these terminal decisions especially the ones that I helped to put into motion from the start.

I should also note that once that final decision was made my life got significantly less stressful, and I slept better. That doesn't mean I didn't feel the loss and regret the process I approved and then had to terminate but the resulting decision always cleared the air and allowed for progress of other programs that had suffered with my preoccupation with the prior program decision. In all cases, no one quit when they were overloaded and down. Instead, they stopped, or pivoted, into something that had a better opportunity for success.

The Lesson

When you make a proper decision based on the information available to you and you want the effort to succeed, you have to pay the price to carry the idea to a successful conclusion. If instead, you realize, for a variety of reasons that that decision was not the best choice, you need to take immediate action to correct the situation since you now realize you are using resources that could be better used in other applications.

I have had several occasions where I have had to change the direction of the original decision, or the project in general, to better utilize the resources at hand. When I had those occasions, one of the songs that plays in my mind is from the "The Gambler" sung by Kenny Rogers. I suspect it is that active, but not so silent, part of my brain that reminds me that while I have made some wise decisions in my career, I have also made some…well, you know.

The song has a lot of words, but these four lines do it for me. The reality is that once you make a proper decision, you have committed yourself to the successful conclusion of the project, even when it starts to look hopeless or you have overextended yourself. Remember, you made a commitment through your decision-making. But if the decision now needs to be redefined, changed, or eliminated, then you need to at least walk, if not run, from the bad situation. I hope the words of this song helps you as much as it has me.

The Gambler

> You've got to know when to hold 'em
> Know when to fold 'em
> Know when to walk away
> And know when to run

The Role of Scientists and Engineers

The stewardship of both innovation and leadership determines the rate of advancement of a society, the lack thereof its decay.

Personal Experience

This section has been placed near the end of this book. It effectively combines most of what I learned some in my personal life but mostly from the events and learning processes encountered in my professional life. Some portions of the contents have been repeated here from earlier lessons and hopefully combined into a better perspective. I hope you will appreciate the lessons I learned the hard way but often, more importantly, the best way.

Clearly choosing to be an engineer or a scientist is a personal decision and one that should be considered carefully. There are a lot of disciplines available for each of you to choose from. Each will allow you to make a contribution to our social system and provide the image of yourself you desire and deserve. In each and every discipline, there will be the opportunity to become the leader and/or the innovator. The choice will and should be yours as is the responsibility for the decisions that you will ultimately make.

I speak to these two disciplines in their many forms, primarily because I know them well since I lived them the majority of my professional life. It is also my hope that these words will help you to understand some of the characteristics that engineers and scientists exhibit and are sometimes blamed for. Like an athlete with muscle memory, an engineer and a scientist are affected by what they learn and study. It affects our thought processes and even our personalities. I thought you might want to know a little about these two professions; it might help to add perspective to your thinking.

The Summary

A majority of the more successful companies and enterprises, both domestic and global, were started and driven by the vision, problem-solving and leadership capabilities of its technically trained founders and/or principals. Historically, these entrepreneurial efforts resulted directly from the intellectual power and leadership skill set of the more technically trained, a large percentage of those enterprises coming into existence during a time when an engineering or scientific degree was not necessarily the norm, or completely defined, but where the design, decision-making, and technical training were still essential characteristics, of a type, often directly associated with the science and engineering disciplines of today.

In more recent times, there has been a steady increase in those leadership and entrepreneurial efforts for the trained and degreed scientist and engineer. Since at least the beginning of the last century, it has become clear that the ongoing problems we face in this country, and for that matter, the globe, will require technical solutions, the perfect opportunity for a well-trained scientific and engineering community, especially ones that have developed their global awareness, leadership skills, and the desire to make and leave a lasting legacy through innovation.

Nevertheless, it was with the early rigorously and technically trained individuals where both the leadership instinct and the entrepreneurial spirit seem to have blossomed resulting in the creation of many of the life-changing technology developments we see and use today. Arguably, the question is, did the resulting technical training uncover, develop, or at least heighten the leadership and entrepreneurial skill set of those professionals or are natural leaders drawn to the rigors and often more technical skill set. I suspect it is a mixture of both, often resulting in a technical community with significantly enhanced leadership capabilities and a vision for an improved future that they become driven to achieve.

Whatever the mixture, or the cause, there is a growing number of enterprises that have reconstituted their organizational structure to include technical assets in their decision-making ranks. Governments around the globe are encouraging their technically trained leadership to take a more active role in promulgating their policies and decision-making trees. The governing bodies in this country have also started to recognize the need to increase the technical and leadership competencies within their ranks to better support the entrepreneur and the implementation of the needed technical solutions.

It is unclear at this point, though, whether a critical mass is available that understands the correlation and contrast between the technically trained and technology development, leadership skills and professional training, entrepreneurialism and economic impact, and being a visionary and making the tough decisions; but there is growing evidence that the evolution has started. Needless to say, there is an ever-growing number of situations that will allow our technically skilled the opportunity to serve their local and larger communities. Clearly, it is with strong visionary leadership that an organization can grow and flourish.

Thus, in general, the proliferation of new technologies, one of the primary keys to modern societal growth relies on the development of two individual but highly interrelated competencies, leadership, and innovation, both of which often appear to be well-placed in the technically trained disciplines. These two and the disciplines they result from are the basis for the successful development of most of the major technologies in use today, and at their best, they are also the genesis behind most of the large commercial and industrial organizations currently operating in the global marketplace.

It is the state of health of these two linked competencies that often determine the longevity and profitability of these organizations. The question should then be what role does, and will, the engineer and scientist play in this leadership driven innovation play and how will they continue to help develop and become the architects of our future? Have we done enough and what will scientist and engineers need to do in the future to continue a growth-based legacy?

The Discussion

I believe we should start off this lesson by addressing what should be one of the more important and fundamental questions in our lives. It is most likely one of those same questions that each succeeding generation asks: "What is it that the collective—we—intends to leave as a legacy for our children?" As a species on this planet, we have come a long way. We have managed to effectively subdue our environment and have found a way to live with each other in spite of our growing population density along with our philosophical differences.

In spite of this, we still tend to sensationalize everything around us along with the negative possibilities that are just sitting on the immediate horizon waiting on us to make some fatal mistake. If you pay attention to the popular press, and especially many movie themes, what you get is doom and gloom. Plus, if you add to the mix the future role that advanced technology could play in our demise, then surely, we will all perish in a ball of fire or maybe our heads will simply explode.

For the fun of it, let's look at a few of the more recognizable past beliefs. It hasn't been that many centuries since we could have sailed off the edge of the Earth. In the 1800s, the prevailing thought was that a train moving faster than an animal could run would make us all go mad. In the last century, leaving Earth in a spaceship would alter us genetically or, worse, punch a hole in the atmosphere and let all of the air out. My favorite is, in this century, I am convinced that social media will end life as we know it, or at least make my head explode. There are, of course, hundreds more of these past beliefs that have gone by the wayside and most likely, some of the more current ones will suffer the same lot.

The truth of the matter is, technology serves us not only for our convenience and pleasure; it has also prompted our continued survival. It has allowed us to move the thresholds farther and farther from what could have been survived just centuries ago. It has also put to rest an ever-growing list of unrealistic and unsupportable beliefs, most likely a necessary part of the process with a maturing social order and the associated technical development. For instance, the rest of the universe does not revolve around the Earth, or any of us individually for that matter. Please note, though, that most of my children, during their teenage years, would have disagreed with this last statement.

With respect to our continued survival and societal growth, it is with the medium of energy and the driving forces of innovation and leadership that represent two of the key factors for our success. In addition to these factors is the concept of self-sufficiency, an essential ingredient that makes us stand on our own and reach for ever-increasing heights. It is through technology that we have allowed ourselves to develop creatively and intellectually along with immeasurable advances in our social order.

Price of Progress

Of course, all of this has come at a price that some say is too high and which has presented the following dilemma, at least for some. Should we continue to advance or maybe go back to a simpler time? I, for one, know without question that that simpler time occurred during my childhood, or maybe from one of my fantasies during some medieval time where I could have been a knight in shining armor ready on a moment's notice to rescue a local damsel in distress. I also remember that my dad argued that that simpler time occurred while he was a child or when the Native Americans flourished here.

It turns out that each of us has a preferred simpler time that we reminisce about. The memories of those simpler times are normally devoid of the actual complexities of the day, either through selective memory or just plain dreamer's choice. These notions also make for great story lines in books and movies, but the reality is much more complex and interwoven for us to simply stop and go back to a simpler time.

Think about the consequences of simply slowing down technological progress. It would have unparalleled and dire consequences on us, our society, the environment, and the lists go on. In fact, the very people who suggest that we need to stop technical advances are the ones who use them to advance their causes. I would love to have those technical illiterates' hand over their keys, sever their power lines and, once their batteries run out, shut off their social media.

Embracing Change

The reality is that few people understand the complete picture of the interdependencies that exist within our society and particularly the relationship we have with the environment we live in. Nor do they understand or even know the inventive pathways that allow us to move forward and to make progress in that complex system. Fortunately, there are a few amongst us who do see the bigger picture. These are the few that truly embrace change. For them, it is with the embrace of change where innovative breakthroughs can, and do, occur.

A large percentage of the more aware are the scientists and engineers who seek to solve the complex problems that society generates for all of us. Within this small group, there is an even more specialized group of what are often referred to as the troublemakers, misfits, and non-team players, at least that is what they are considered initially. They are most likely in large measure the innovators that move us forward and provide the timely breakthroughs that have been so historically necessary for our survival.

Key additions to these innovators, along with their passions, are the leaders who drive them and their ideas into the marketplace. In fact, to be truly effective requires both sets of these characteristics. Thus, as is often the case, *the stewardship of both innovation and leadership determines the rate of advancement of a society, the lack thereof its decay.*

All of society had best hope for their continued contributions, or at least they should try to get out of their way. A large percentage of these troublemakers in both camps, let's call them visionaries, are technically trained often as engineers and scientists. They somehow see a different future than do most of us and use the tools of their trade to perpetuate that vision. Most of these types "self-select" their careers and disciplines, as do most scientist and engineers. So they often have little choice in how they react in and with their social environment. While the following list is a bit contentious, scientists and engineers, and the leadership that drives them, are for the most part:

Arguable Characteristics

- Less social (more introverted, less likely to recognize everyday social cues).
- They tend to march to a different drummer (it isn't normally deliberate; it is just who they are).
- Obsessively driven by visions of a better future (tendency for at least mild obsessive-compulsive disorder characteristics).
- Continuously finding solutions to problems the general public doesn't even know exists (in touch with the complex environment they exist in).
- Less inclined to see the world as it is seen by the majority (with matching tunnel vision, which is put down as folly by most of the uninitiated and as part of being overworked by those who care the most for them).
- Finding ways to improve situations that are already regarded as okay (can't stop fixing what others believe isn't broken).
- Even more unlikely to be happy with the final results of their work (perfectionists).
- They also tend to get bored easily (will start anew, probably on something totally unrelated to their previous work).

As for those that care the most for these individuals, I feel a special sympathy, and this is particular true for the significant others who share their lives. For instance, my wife constantly tells me that all scientists and engineers are weird, are impossible to live with, and who just can't leave well enough alone. Then, in the next breath, she will ask me to go and fix a piece of technology she will refer to as a thingy.

These visionaries are often called risk-takers and seemingly independent or oblivious to mainstream thought. The truth is that they don't have an absence of risk; they just have a much higher threshold, or even more likely, they don't understand the term.

As far as thinking outside of the box, well, they have been given way too much credit for this characteristic. They are normally oblivious to the actual workings of the social order they exist in and, fortunately for all of us, the reality is that they just couldn't find the box everyone else uses as the standard.

Innovation and Leadership Value

Can we, in fact, overstress the value of innovation and leadership and the role they play when combined for the benefit of mankind and nature? I don't think so. It turns out we are the most successful macro-species on the planet. As mentioned earlier, this is in a large part because we are inventive, innovative, and in our best state, self-sufficient with the leadership driven vision to push through to the end. We rise to the occasion when threatened and we continuously help to generate a pool of creative, intelligent, and consciously driven decision-makers, the next generation.

When as younger individuals this next generation becomes technically trained enough to start making contributions to the society that has helped to raise and train them, and the visionary leadership is so inclined, we get changes and solutions at a rate to meet our problems and needs. Albeit it is often not with the timing that we would all like, but once they set their sights on the solution, they will become a force of nature. Some of their problem solutions will be evolutionary and some revolutionary. All will go through a maturation process to get to the marketplace, or in many more cases, they just won't make it successfully, at least not the first time.

To be an innovation requires that the invention mature into a marketable solution. It also requires a level of leadership backing that idea, commensurate with the disruptive nature of the invention, all supported by the technical trained. Sometimes, the key elements just don't come together. For instance, some of the successes, and also the failures, are in the timing. More is in the heart and the passion of the creators, leaders, and sponsors. The rest is with consumer or end-user acceptance.

History shows how some of the most innovative technologies were from the start doomed to failure but for the persistence of the creators and their leaders and sponsors. Note that the more potentially disruptive the solution, the harder it will be to get to a successful market no matter how valuable the future will determine the end result.

So if all of this is at least slightly true, why are we in the current state we are in? Are we even in a state that needs to be changed? If the innovation process is such that when we need change, the white knight will appear to save the day, then why all of the current fuss about innovation, or the lack thereof?

The Fuss over Innovation

One of the contentions of this lesson is that society and its needs are evolving at an ever-increasing rate. What used to be generational problems, those recognized in time for the youth to be educated about and then to spend their careers into retirement solving, are now problems that need to be fixed by at least Friday after next, just in time for the next crisis. We no longer have the luxury of waiting for visionaries to arrive to save the day; we now need to help find them and to provide the tools to encourage their growth and productivity.

All the while, we will need to stay out of their way, remaining ready to catch their next hair-brained idea, to drive it into the marketplace if it is good enough. What we need to force recognition of is that the subset of the population that have the requisite attributes to be visionaries is much greater than is currently understood or accepted. They are all around us, and most of them are among the young.

It turns out that the current system has not exposed or allowed them to develop the requisite skill sets they might need to break out and do innovative things. What, you might ask, are some of the roadblocks we have thrown in front of our youth and the public in general? A few of the roadblocks are the following:

Roadblocks to Our Future

- An educational system that celebrates and requires uniformity (encouraging mediocrity),
- A terribly uninformed and misdirected media
- A technically trained but underrepresented group in our governance functions at all levels

Fortunately, a good many of these future visionaries will self-select into disciplines that might allow them to flourish. What we really have to worry about, then, is the inertia from the misinformation that constantly surrounds us, somewhat like the "sailing off the edge" statement from earlier in this lesson.

The failure to create a clear and technically accurate picture of our situation has fragmented our understanding of the number and severity of the problems that actually need to be handled. It has also diluted our attention and our willingness to rally support and to focus our energies as a united populace.

There are probably hundreds of additional reasons that could be added to the above list, all equally important to someone, but outside of the scope of this discussion. What needs to be noted is that the general public is not the reason for a lack of innovation. They tend to embrace change, although the older individuals among us may have more reluctance: back to the social media issue and my exploding brain.

We all want to have the next best thing, want to be fashionable, often unknowingly, we may also try to keep up with the neighbors, plus, we always want to improve our lot and chances for survival. The reality is that features only buy us so much. It is the benefits that solve the problems, and we are clearly due for some real change, most likely a long list of potential breakthroughs.

Fixing the Problems

How are we to get to those changes and how do we make it happen on a timelier and possibly predictable basis? The answer is buried in the question. The answer sits with the word "*we*" as in "*We have to do it.*"

Sitting in hundreds of laboratories, shops, and offices all around the world are some of the most talented and technically skilled professionals that our current civilization has fostered. Getting to this skilled state, through the rigors of education and experience, and all of the constraints that had to be worked around, has provided this trained group with immense insight.

In other words, they have learned where all the minefields are. It would not be hard to argue that with all these presented opportunities comes an even greater set of personal responsibilities and obligations, as if scientists and engineers don't already have enough to do. Clearly, most of these technical types do feel a pressure to contribute either due the opportunities given them or because they see the need a little better.

Yes, I almost hear the complaints from this group: there are too many rules and restrictions, no one listens, and there are way too many problems, we are not paid enough, and our job descriptions do not include that next "whatever," plus society expects too much, rewards too little, and often holds us too responsible for the outcomes, when they don't do what was recommended.

Does any of this really matter? Like the majority of the engineers and scientists, visionaries do self-select, and they are who they are no matter how society tries to conform them. While there may be medicines to help cover some of their symptoms, they really tend to be well-grounded (in their own way) and quite happy doing what they do, often indifferent of what goes on around them and independent of the accepted thoughts of the day.

The question is, is this enough? I believe that with the rate of change that is running us to ground, we no longer have the luxury of expecting someone else to handle those things we currently think are outside of our purview. Scientists and engineers need to take a more aggressive role in our society in a variety of ways. The first is to recognize that the problems we see are most likely not seen or understood by the general public, who for the record are at the mercy of the media and their own limited perspective and understanding. Second, the potential solutions visionary's might choose are also subject to the same scrutiny as above, but they are also affected by special interests, their own personal prejudices, and the constraints of surviving the rigors of everyday life.

It is because of what is expected, often demanded from them, that scientists and engineers should give society what they may not really want, but desperately need: the facts, the reality attached to those facts, and the process needed to implement the best solutions.

On top of all of this, which could be considered a disruptive innovation in itself, is the need to bootstrap the next generation of leaders and innovators. They are all around us, and they need our help desperately. I know because I have spent my career working with them. Learning to mentor the next great visionary, and their contribution, is not only satisfying, but it will also add perspective and a legacy moment to everyone's career.

On top of making an important contribution to someone's success, there is an even more important use of scientist's and engineer's time, providing the factual information the rest of the world needs to make better-informed decisions that will, in the end, help us all. Thus, I leave you with my version of an innovation/leadership challenge.

The Innovation/Leadership Challenge

- Engineers and scientists must become the agents for change: adaptive, supportive, and disruptive.
- Engineers and scientists must incorporate innovation as their philosophy to be used as a tool to set policy for technological, cultural, and societal change.

- Engineers and scientists must learn to communicate effectively and to provide consensus based technical support for policy decisions.
- Engineers and scientists need to find and mentor that next great set of visionaries, the innovators along with the leadership needed to make them successful.

From my reference point, these individuals are most likely predominately within the ranks of our youth. It is with them that we are leaving the problems that were created when we solved the problems from our earlier days. They are the ones living with these problems, and most likely, they see them better and from the correct vantage point for the future. They also have the most energy and passion to address them but lack the experience and resources to easily face the challenges or to make the needed changes. We can, and must, help them make that transition.

The Lesson

If you choose, or have chosen, to become a scientist, an engineer, or a member of the leadership community that will ultimately drive innovation, more power to you. The world needs many more of you, plus the innovative individuals than we currently recognize and help develop. The world we live in is at its best with a diverse set of interests and talents. As a social order matures the balance in all of the needed disciplines will change, but the responsibilities of the overall population should never change; the creation and protection of the social and physical environments that extends our survival.

We, each in our own way, need to accept the responsibilities of our decisions and actions and always question the status quo. The only constant in the universe is change, and as such, if we aren't seeing it, then we are the ones at fault. Observe, learn, and always try to make a contribution to your own future, the ones around you, and especially the ones to come in the future.

My Failed Retirement

It's not what you don't know, but rather what you don't know that you don't know that will get you in the end.

The Discussion

I had considered and discussed with my family the notion of retirement for years prior to actually pulling that trigger. I was getting older, clearly past the accepted retirement age and seemingly not up to the rigors of the job, most of those rigors had been self-imposed. All of my children had flown the coop years earlier and were in their own ways providing the next set of problems for me and my wife to handle, grandchildren.

As the sole bread winner for the family, I assumed the role of making sure the bills were paid and most of the wants for the family were handled, or at least seriously considered. I had looked forward to retirement because, well, that is part of the working man's process. I did have some ideas about retirement and had thought through a series of events and possibilities of what I might do with the extra time afforded by a retirement. Note that most of those plans have either been forgotten, evaporated, or displaced by more important issues.

On top of this was some pending medical issues that couldn't be fixed but could be managed if I wasn't too stubborn or in denial. Also, I had an opportunity to work with a technology start-up, and that was something I really wanted to do. I, of course, assumed, and you know what assuming does, that working with this new company would allow me the flexibility and time to pursue other interests: wife, family, hobbies, travel, etc.

Since I pride myself on making effective and well-thought-out decisions, you would have thought I had all of this under control. Let me explain my misunderstanding of the actual situation and the direct consequences of my decisions, and sometimes lack of decisions. At first, I had plenty to do, there were a lot of honey-do jobs that had been put off until retirement. I sure wish I hadn't put off so many of those boring jobs.

I also had a company to help manage and while the technology was extremely exciting the owners had unrealistic expectations and some had personal designs on the outcome of the company. This provided another opportunity for a second retirement and also another list of honey-do jobs to do. This is when I finally started to understand my actual situation.

It seems as I was doing my second set of honey-do jobs, that my wife started to find me annoying, and I couldn't for the life of me understand the problem. As I explained it to her, I had spent the previous forty-plus years, also the length of our marriage at that point, going to a job. During all of that time, I missed seeing my wife and kids while at work, and now I had the time to spend quality time with whoever was available, by default, the wife.

This is when she said the following: "For the past forty years, I have had to fair on my own, maintaining a house, raising our four kids, and always keeping the house ready for your return in the evenings. I would normally see you in the evening and on weekends, and I got adjusted to that routine and have managed to make a life around that schedule. I had about forty to sixty hours a week to take care of the things that needed my attention, including the things I needed to do for me. Now, nothing is getting done and my outside activities, crafts, and hobbies, have come to an end. You have to go back to work." Whereupon, she presented me some clippings from the local newspaper want ads, including a call for a greeter at one of the local convenience stores.

Truth be told, I felt like a caged beast that wanted to get back to work anyway. I had worked for over 70 percent of my life, the majority of which was fulltime. I hadn't missed the professorial job, except for the interaction with the energetic young people, but I did miss the mental stimulation and efforts to create and move technology forward. So I was offered and took a job as an intellectual property advisor for a couple of companies and I have also settled in to drafting several manuscripts, one of which is this one and its predecessor.

Note that my wife is happier now, and we even get together during the workday for lunches and outings, but infrequently. I am allowed to even get interested in her hobbies as long as I don't make suggestions on how to improve her creative arts.

The Lesson

The lesson here might not be evident to the younger reader since age and experience, especially marriage, will help with your understanding. It turns out that most people can't stop doing what they have been doing for most of a lifetime. There are a lot of ingrained habits that are established to help manage the work effort, which also impacts who and what the person will become.

Until age and health overcome us as individuals, we all need to continue doing what made us who we are. I was always told, when I was younger, that if a person stops doing scheduled activities after they retire, then they will not last long in this world. I now understand this thought. Not working and making a contribution was creating stress levels greater than the ones I suffered through when I worked. More importantly my wife is much happier now.

Epilogue

*If this book brings you value,
We will both be the better for it.*

Discussion

This book covered a lot of the lessons that affected my professional career and by association also my personal life. Some of it had relatable stories while others most likely were rather technical in nature, if not also obscure. It is my belief that each of you will encounter similar stories with resulting lessons, albeit different based on your career path and the other choices in your life. While the specific details will be uniquely different, it is my belief that there will be a common theme from these stories in what you learn as you work through your specific lessons.

Remember, these stories have been told by someone who has been highly influenced by the career choices and the visionary path that I walked. This most likely affects the way the story ultimately is told, but more than likely, the results are similar in content and effect to the stories you will experience.

To assist with the diverse areas covered in this book, the following is a list to remind you of the most important aspects of the lessons in this book. It will also help you to find a specific lesson should you need a reminder or want to use the same in discussions with friends, family, and colleagues.

Lesson Takeaways

1. "Goal Setting." Life is an ongoing, living process; and every action, or lack of one, contributes to that process. Like any puzzle, the pieces that will finally constitute the makings of your life must all come together to fit properly for the image you require. Remember you control the goals, pathway, and ultimately, the final image.
2. "Focus on the Prize." Be vigilant in your approach in solving life's problems by avoiding, or ignoring, its many distractions and make it your intent to seize the day at every turn, for the rest of your life.
3. "Financial Security." Your financial security is your goal to define. It is also your responsibility to choose the best and most effectively path to get to that preferred image of yourself. More importantly, it is for you to decide if it is the dog or the tail that is doing the wagging. In other words, you choose the contents of the goal, don't let others do it for you.
4. "The Advertised Expert." Never settle for a cursory understanding of the roles and responsibilities, plus the motivation of the individuals, in any positions of authority or who are presented as experts. Personal accolades, employment titles, and agency stations along with advertised program offices are not necessarily as they are represented. Always dig deeper and if their value to you is still in question, move on to the next opportunity. There are too many opportunities for you to worry about any that might get away or are in question.
5. "Age and Treachery." We need to not only support our young innovators with word and deed but to also stay out of their way, making sure others do the same. They have the youth and vigor to make things happen. The older veterans have the age and experience to steer the best and safest course to success. It is the union of both groups that will allow the most successes in the future.

6. "Jobs versus Wealth." Wealth creation draws out the creative people who might normally go unnoticed. The currently used employment numbers model draws out small business developers, which while important, often exclude the person with the future game changing technology. Creating wealth is the best way to improve your life and society in general.
7. "Can't Never Done Nothing." The key is to never let your lack of understanding about who is ultimately responsible for a decision determine who and what you will become. Even more importantly, you never want to let someone else be the decision-maker in your life.
8. "Directed Action: Goals." A goal is the thing that you plan to do or achieve as if it is already an established determination. In other words, you have worked out the details and required processes to the point that the goal will effectively happen by its own volition. Bumps in the road will be handled through your prior planning or they can be smoothed out with the contingencies you have set aside for all of your visionary plans.
9. "You in Five Years." A personal vision for the future is possibly one of the strongest attributes that should be established early in a person's life and career and then acted on continuously for the rest of that life.
10. "Knowing Your Direction." Once you select your goals and have chosen the pathway to those goals, it is your responsibility to stay on course to that intended destination. All of this is in fact your choice and you are ultimately responsible for the outcome.
11. "Clawing to Success." In lots of cases, the failure of a new activity, enterprise, or innovative program is not from too little capital but in fact the opposite. It seems that when you are capital rich, you tend to design, develop, or service what you want in contrast to providing what the customer needs. Remember to always satisfy the needs of the customer. They most likely don't care about your wants.

12. "Three Types of Decisions." There are three types of decisions: *the correct one*, *the incorrect one*, and *the lack of one*. The first, we celebrate; the second, we learn from; and the last we are to admonish, for it steals our spirit and delays, and sometimes denies, our progress.
13. "My Admission." Over the course of my long career, and specifically even more so now, I have come to accept, and thus need to come clean, two admissions regarding what I believe and have tried to convey in my classroom, laboratory, and personal life. First, when dealing with the real world, which has yet to be fully defined, half of what I have been teaching and practicing is incorrect. The second admission is that I don't know which half.
14. "Mankind and Energy: That's Why." The only constant in life is change. It is through our increasing knowledge and the use of the energy around us that we will be able to continue human progress in the future.
15. "Workplace Friendships." Never let the lure of friendship dictate the course of your future goals or your career. True friends are just as concerned and would not put you into a position where your livelihood would be put into question.
16. "Find the Cure." We have become a society focused on the symptoms of our problems and, along with it, finger-pointing at who and what are causing our problems. We are the problems and of course also the solutions. We are all responsible for future outcomes. Time to assume that responsibility and get down to work.
17. "Energy: Our Economic Indicator." For those of you looking for a new career path or just starting your career, the most likely success stories will come from the energy sector and any innovation that uses that energy or makes its use more acceptable, efficient, and affordable.
18. "The Missing Link." What makes us so successful is our ability to establish a goal and with the right leadership form up into a formidable force to get something completed. A chain is a terrible tool for pushing but when led properly

it is unrelenting in its ability to pull us to where we need to go.

19. "Is There Anything New?" For those who argue that it has already been invented or studied or written and produced, you have missed out on one of the most important attributes of our species—a hopeful view of the future, along with the ability to create the innovations that will get us there. If you are not going to be part of the latest innovations, then at least get out of the way of those who will.

20. "What Are They against This Time?" Opposing viewpoints are critical to any reasonable decision-making process but sometimes the counterpoints have little or no basis in fact or science, relying only on emotional arguments that often have little or no basis in reality. Learn the facts and manage your emotional influences.

21. "It's Not What You Don't Know." "It's not what you don't know but rather what you don't know that you don't know that will get you in the end."

22. "Innovation: Will You See It." I see a visionary drive in the young people that I have had the privilege to work with. I hear it in the language they use and the vision of the future they expect to create. Why not join them, the ride will be exciting and full of wonder.

23. "Changing Cycles." Life may begin at the edge of the comfort zone, but familiarity and predictability beg to extend the illusion that life can be made a little more controllable; albeit more boring. Some people simply ignore the reality that change will continue to happen no matter what we choose to believe. It is for us to embrace change as part of the natural cycle of life.

24. "Science and Technology." The value of science and the advancements in technology are immeasurable, unpredictable, and often unimaginable. Without them, though, the current global social order and our ability to sustain human life would be at best, marginal. It is through these crafted capabilities that we will continue to advance mankind in

ways that only the philosophers and fiction writers can foretell.

25. Assuming there are no catastrophic or cataclysmic events on our horizon, it would be fair to assume we will find the solutions to the never-ending problems that we continuously create, as a result of solving some previous set of problems. Thus, life will go on and the social order will advance through the myriad of endless possibilities, most likely perpetuated on the advancements created through science and technology.

26. "The Virtual Commercialization Model." The virtual commercialization model is upon us. For those of you already participating in these new venues, congratulations and welcome to the future in entrepreneurism. For those of you who haven't tuned in yet, I hope you will decide to catch up with what's going on all around you, even if it is later.

27. "Too Many Words." In most all situations, a well-planned activity will result in less words, often making excuses or pointing fingers unnecessary. In all cases, it will take far less words to provide a preferred positive outcome or a recommendation for a different path to the same or similar outcome.

28. "Stop Doing Stupid." Isn't it time for each of us to identify a small piece of the ever-present human foolishness so we can help to improve the same? In other words, it's time to *stop doing stupid*, independent of who is doing it because if we don't identify and try to correct it when it happens, then we are guilty of perpetuating that foolishness, making it even worse downstream.

29. "The Innovation/Leadership Impulse." We all have the leadership instinct. We also have the desire to improve the situations around us through innovation. Remember, *leadership without innovation promotes the short term while neglecting the future. Innovation without leadership is undirected, needlessly expending resources while eroding stakeholder*

value. With both you get vision, planning, and confidence to overcome the hurdles brought on by progress and change.

30. "Managing Committees." Always look to the committee charge when asked to join a committee. If it appears management is looking for the information needed to make a responsible decision, then most likely it is a good use of your time.

31. "Economic Indicators." To stay ahead in this world will mean a movement back to maverick, shoot from the hip, innovative genius that we used to look for and reward and still have buried in the hearts of our next generation leaders and innovators. By the way, you are that next generation.

32. "Future Mobility Drivers." We are all effectively energy in one form or another, and we use energy external from our bodies to pursue those activities related to our survival and continued social development. If you want to be productive in your short stay on this planet, you will need to understand your personal role in, and potential contributions to, this total energy process.

33. "Never Quit When You Are Down." Make your commitments through your decision-making. Know when to change those decisions and don't hesitate in that decision.

34. "The Role of Scientists and Engineers." We, each in our own way, need to accept the responsibilities of our decisions and actions and always question the status quo. The only constant in the universe is change, and as such, if we aren't seeing change, then we are the ones at fault. Observe, learn, and always try to make a contribution through your choices in life and the decisions you will inevitably have to make. This will be essential for your own future, the ones around you, and especially the ones to come in the future.

35. "My Failed Retirement." Life starts and ends in an unpredictable fashion. It is for us to choose our path and to stay true to its course. Once established, all habits that allow for your personal expression should be cultivated and made a part of your future until your effectiveness in this life has

ended. The experience you gain doing life's essentials will always have value to someone. Become useful in all aspects of your life.

Closure

Clearly, this book covered a broad range of topics. Some resulted from personal development issues while others covered the interactions and impact of the events constantly occurring daily all around each of us. I hope you will use the lessons contained here to reflect on your own learned lessons and the ones you will most likely encounter in the future. If any of the contents in this book brings you value or if it causes you to at least smile a little due to a similar experience you have had, we will all be the better for it. Thank you for the giving of your time to this reading.

About the Author

James E. Smith, PhD, is a retired university professor with forty-five-plus years of experience as a practicing engineer and educator. During his career, he has taken on the roles of an engineer, corporate consultant, research center director, and professor. These professional roles have satisfied his need to stay connected to his engineering profession, but with retirement, his focus has shifted to providing what he has learned over the years to those who might have need for such hard-earned knowledge. His recent interests have shifted to writing and creating new consumer products. The writing efforts have resulted in a book on leadership, *The Leadership Instinct—Leading Yourself Out of Social Mediocrity*, and a first book on life's lessons, *Life's Little Lessons—with Some Not So Little*. These other product development endeavors, if successful, might eventually become parts to a new *Life's Little Lessons* series.

Currently, during his infrequent downtimes, he is especially active in chasing after grandchildren and the operation of a "gentleman's" farm where he and his wife look after deer and wild turkey, plus an occasional meandering bear. Their four children visit at will but are particularly attentive when they need to borrow something or wish to leave their offspring to their parents' designs. The four children he and his wife raised survived and flourished, so it is assumed that as grandparents, they can handle the next generation hopefully as well as inexpensive babysitters. This, again, may become part of another life's little lessons for the future, if they, the older generation, survive the energetic set of munchkins left to their designs. Grandkids are such a blessing, and grandparents frequently look forward to their visits, but they often feel the same way with their departures.